HERBERT JACOB
Northwestern University

crime
and
justice
in
urban
america

Prentice-Hall, Inc., *Englewood Cliffs, New Jersey 07632*

Library of Congress Cataloging in Publication Data

JACOB, HERBERT (date)
    Crime and justice in urban America.

    Includes bibliographical references and index.
    1. Criminal justice, Administration of—United
States.   2. Criminal courts—United States.
3. Municipal courts—United States.   4. Law and
politics.   I. Title.
KF9223.J33   364'.973   79–14106
ISBN 0–13–192849–X

For Jenny and Max

Printed in the United States of America

10   9   8   7   6   5   4   3   2   1

Editorial/production supervision
and interior design by Lynda Heideman
Cover design by Allyson Everngam
Manufacturing Buyer: Harry P. Baisley

PRENTICE-HALL INTERNATIONAL, INC., *London*
PRENTICE-HALL OF AUSTRALIA PTY. LIMITED, *Sydney*
PRENTICE-HALL OF CANADA, LTD., *Toronto*
PRENTICE-HALL OF INDIA PRIVATE LIMITED, *New Delhi*
PRENTICE-HALL OF JAPAN, INC., *Tokyo*
PRENTICE-HALL OF SOUTHEAST ASIA PTE. LTD., *Singapore*
WHITEHALL BOOKS LIMITED, *Wellington, New Zealand*

contents

6

criminal justice in new york, chicago, los angeles, and prairie city
97

7

conflict, the law, and city politics
127

8

dispute processing in american cities
145

9

variations in concluding civil conflicts: a closer look at four wisconsin cities
167

preface

This book is a successor to *Urban Justice*.[1] I wrote the previous book on the eve of my research on the ways in which felony defendants were processed by the courts of Baltimore, Chicago, and Detroit. That research, coauthored with James Eisenstein, has since been published under the title *Felony Justice* and informs much of what I have now written on the criminal prosecution process.[2] At the same time, there has been an enormous outpouring of research on criminal justice, and this book reflects that new research. We now know, for instance, that plea bargaining is not simply the consequence of heavy caseloads; it existed long before such pressures developed in urban courts and even now flourishes in jurisdictions with light caseloads. We also know that there is little overt discrimination against blacks in criminal courts. Nevertheless, because blacks are more often charged with serious crimes and possess prior criminal records, they more often receive severe sentences. We know that sentences vary tremendously from city to city and sometimes even within a city from one judge to another. It is not at all clear, however, that plea bargaining softens penalties. Finally, we have overwhelming evidence that public defenders do as good a job representing their clients as private attorneys, although clients feel they are better represented when they pay for their own counsel rather than depend on the public defender.

We have also learned a great deal from victimization surveys about the incidence of crime and from criminological studies about the characteristics of offenders. These studies show that the young — not the elderly—are the most vulnerable group of victims. They also show that criminal careers peak at a relatively early age in most instances so that few persons persist in crime beyond the age of thirty-five.

We have also learned a little bit about the ways in which civil justice operates in American cities. Here the poor are greatly disadvantaged. The have-nots operate under severe handicaps both in defending themselves against evictions (see the story of Chicago's housing court in chapter 8) and against debt collectors. Prominent cases involving issues such as freedom of the press or school integration catch public attention and are important in a city's political life; the humdrum conflicts concerning individual citizens rarely attract public attention, but they also affect a community's well-being.

The link between politics and court decisions is often obscure and indirect. Sometimes the only link is the fact that courts are governmental institutions that can be directed to favor one group or another. Sometimes, however, courts directly intervene in political disputes (as in election cases), and sometimes they are the source of large amounts of patronage in the form of jobs and services. To ignore their work is to lack a complete understanding of a city's political life.

I wrote this book on the eve of another substantial research undertaking. With Professor Robert Lineberry, I am now examining the rise of crime since World War II in American cities and governmental responses to it. In this book I express my doubts about the effectiveness of city policies in combating crime, but little hard evidence exists to substantiate either such doubts or the counterclaims of government agencies that they have succeeded in stemming the crime wave of the 1970s. In five years I hope to be able to present the evidence that will indicate which view is correct.

I am as always deeply indebted to many researchers for the evidence reported in this book; I acknowledge them in the notes and trust that I have presented their findings fairly. I am also indebted to my colleagues at Northwestern University for providing an intellectual climate in which writing and research can be successfully combined with teaching. I especially want to acknowledge the comments on portions of this manuscript made by Robert L. Lineberry and Wesley G. Skogan as well as the many helpful conversations with Jerry Goldman. My students in a series of law and politics courses have unknowingly contributed by their healthy skepticism and torrent of questions. Finally, my student assistant, Susan Barth, has been an invaluable typist. Whatever errors remain are mine alone.

—————————————————————— **notes** ——————————————————————

1 Herbert Jacob, *Urban Justice* (Englewood Cliffs, N.J.: Prentice-Hall, Inc., 1973).

2 James Eisenstein and Herbert Jacob, *Felony Justice* (Boston, Mass.: Little, Brown & Company, 1977).

justice
and politics

*r*arely do people think of justice as a municipal problem. They seek justice wherever they live, be it in a big city, in a small town, or out in the country. But most Americans now live in cities, and city life substantially complicates the pursuit of justice. Moreover, the quest for justice illustrates many of the problems that characterize urban life, city politics, and municipal government. Among these problems are the activities of interest groups, the competition for funds and advantageous treatment, the transformation of real problems into symbolic crusades, and the tangle of government levels, agencies, and districts.

Justice is foremost a political problem. It requires fair play and the fair treatment of people. We usually presume that it also means the equal treatment of all persons regardless of their social or political connections. Fairness and equality are vague terms that must be given concrete meaning through decisions to allocate valued resources to particular persons. They mean being attentive to claims by citizens against each other and against the government. They mean giving additional clout to those who are poor and taking clout away from those who are wealthy in order to equalize the power each exerts. They mean the blind, evenhanded administration of rules. In a world of scarcities, however, providing for some means disadvantaging others. Thus, some neighborhoods will receive more police protection and others will get less. One set of litigants may be treated more harshly than others; for example, divorce courts may demand more of husbands than of wives. While the rules may be administered evenhandedly, they are themselves the product of political conflict and usually confer advantages or liabilities to certain persons. The rules come from the political arena—from legislatures or city councils. They reflect contemporary political preferences and momentary domination by particular interests. Moreover, the way the rules are carried out has political consequences because it furthers or hinders the careers of political leaders, creates or solves problems for them, and helps mold the agenda of issues under public consideration.

As we shall see throughout this book, the political activities surrounding the administration of justice do not attract widespread media attention. The political events most followed by the media, like election campaigns, seldom have much significance for the courts. One can rarely find argument, conflict, or compromise displayed in the dramatic fashion that is typical of city council proceedings or the activities of a mayor. What we find instead is the quiet activity of interest groups who seek to influence outcomes by backstage maneuvering over the structure and staffing of the courts or by litigation in particular conflicts. However quiet these activities may be, they remain political.

There is nothing dishonorable in pointing to the political character of justice. Indeed, we would be very concerned if it were nonpolitical because such justice would mean that a self-appointed elite controlled the distribution of important values. Because justice is political, those active in the political arena have opportunities to influence the distribution of material and symbolic values through the legal process. Because justice is political, it can be used to promote social goals such as equality, to enforce standards of conduct for officials and private citizens, to reduce exploitation by lenders, landlords, and monopolies, or to improve environmental quality. It is also often used to achieve the opposite goals.

The administration of justice is also often closely intertwined with a city's political life for other reasons. The careers of many city political leaders are shaped by court decisions about their actions. If they or their subordinates are accused of corruption, the outcome of those charges is determined in the hallways and courtrooms of the local courthouse. Challenges to nomination papers and referendum petitions typically go to court. Many careers have been advanced or stopped by a local-court decision on such matters. Decisions by mayors and other political leaders on zoning alterations for large construction projects, on hiring minorities in city jobs, and on cutting services are only some of the many issues that often come to court during some phase of the controversy. Judges usually do not make the final decision, but their voice is one of many affecting the development of public policy in the city.

Justice is not simply a public and political process. It is closely intertwined with decisions made in the private sector. Many of the standards of conduct enforced in courts originate in private usages that gradually have won widespread acceptance; they become "common law" usages and enforceable in court as such. Public laws are often empty vessels that may be filled by whatever content private parties agree upon. For instance, it is public policy that contractual agreements can be enforced except when they violate some specific public policy. Whatever private parties agree on becomes publicly enforceable even though no public official or institution participated. Thus, rental agreements—if they are within the general standards set by law—are enforceable. An agreement between a landlord and tenant may include provisions about pets; another agreement may include provisions about the use of the premises as an artist's studio. Both agreements would be enforceable. Almost all property transactions and many other interactions are put into legally binding form. When conflicts later arise about the interpretation or administration of such agreements, people call upon the justice system to decide. That involves justice agencies in all areas of the economy and in many family and other social relationships that we otherwise consider to be private rather than public. Thus, public and private often interact.

The quest for justice involves the search for both material and symbolic values. Winning a case in court may produce millions of dollars. For instance, a dispute over a contract with the city to run the concessions at an airport may mean the difference between staying in business or going bankrupt for the concessionaire. A favorable decision over the interpretation of zoning laws may allow a developer thousands of additional dollars each month in rent, while loss of the decision may make it financially unfeasible to build the project. Even small consumer disputes center on the payment of monetary sums that, though seemingly small, are large enough for the disputants to bring the matter to court. Disputes that reach the courts often involve more than money, however; they become transformed into conflicts over symbolic values. People bring apparently petty disputes to the legal system because they want an affirmation that they are right, that they acted morally, and that their claims are legitimate. They want not only payment but also moral vindication. Sometimes, as when a group seeks a court order to stop abortions or to halt the distribution of what they consider to be pornographic literature or some gambling activity, the litigants seek only moral affirmation. People who go to court on such issues often have no monetary stake in the outcome. Rather, they feel that their beliefs are being threatened, and they seek from the courts an affirmation of their moral superiority over their adversaries. Thus, much litigation is not a cold commercial transaction but an emotional battle. Much of the ritual associated with trials is intended to stifle the passions that motivate many of the cases brought to court.

Regardless of whether people seek money (material goals) or moral affirmation, they compete for scarce goods when they go to court. Sometimes, compromises satisfy both parties as when someone injured in an auto accident accepts 75 percent of the original claim. That compensation pays all the bills, but at the same time the insurance company does not need to compromise its standards for adjusting claims. At other times, however, compromises are not possible; this is particularly true when symbolic values are at stake. Compromises rarely satisfy litigants who seek moral vindication.

In addition, the justice system itself must compete for scarce resources with other government agencies and programs. The courts must compete for budgetary allocations with the police, the schools, the street department, and all the other government activities in cities. Public officials must choose between more courts and more schools or more sanitation workers or more street repairs.

justice in the city

The quest for justice is very much influenced by the urban character of American life. The characteristics of American cities affect the way legal processes work. Cities are not just the places where courts are located. They are also the social processes that generate the peculiar conflicts that become the agendas for urban courts.

BIG CITIES

City conjures up the image of the sprawling metropolis that has become the dominant feature of American life since World War II. Two-thirds of all Americans now live in metropolitan areas. The conditions that face these urban Americans are quite varied, however.

For some, the big city means the central city, the core of a metropolitan area. It is the oldest part of the metropolis. Most of these cities are old, with deteriorating private and public facilities. Industry is leaving them; downtown shopping centers are dead; the housing supply is dwindling and its quality is deteriorating. Schools, parks, hospitals, and other public facilities are worse now than they were a generation ago.

In most places, the central city is the city of the poor. Concentrated here are blacks, Latinos, Appalachian whites, and other recent arrivals to the city. They live in dilapidated housing, receive poor services, and are highly dependent on public agencies. Many are unemployed because fewer industries require unskilled labor; the new capital-intensive factories need skilled workers and have usually opened in the suburbs out of the reach of the inner-city workers. Many of these persons live in broken families, often headed by the woman. Such areas—stretching across dozens of scores of blocks in cities like Chicago, Los Angeles, or New York—breed intense problems for the justice system. Not only are they high-crime areas, but they are also places where people are easily exploited by landlords and creditors. These areas lack stable private social institutions to reduce or arbitrate private conflicts, so many disputes go to court if they are resolved at all.

But central cities are more than slums. Every large city has sizable areas of middle-class housing and pockets of affluence. Indeed, most of the city more closely resembles the respectable suburbs than the feared slums. Here live the residents who hold the remaining blue-collar jobs in the city. Here are the clerks who staff corporate headquarters and city hall. In some cities these sections still constitute a majority of the population, but it is a psychologically distressed majority. These areas also pose problems for the justice system, but they are of a different magnitude than those posed by the slums. When these people speak of the fear of crime, they often mean the fear that the crime in the other end of town may spread to their neighborhood. They are less concerned with fraud than are slum residents. They use the legal system more often to their own advantage than in response to the threats imposed by others.

Suburbs surround the central cities. Each suburb is a politically independent unit although each depends very much on all the others for its economic viability. Most suburbs are more homogeneous than the central cities in their composition, but they vary greatly among themselves. Many metropolitan areas have suburbs that are as poor as the poorest slum in the central city. Many match the middle-class neighborhoods that dominate the inner city; only a few are islands of affluence. Suburbs face their own problems. They usually do not have the broad tax base of the central cities. Some face the problem of building new schools and other facilities to cope with rapid population growth; others (sometimes in the same metropolitan area) must close schools and cut back services because their population is declining. Because suburbs are usually small, they are more sharply affected by their neighbors' actions and decisions. Unlike the central city, no suburb has a decisive voice in metropolitan-wide governmental bodies such as the prosecutor's office or the county courts.

The problems generated by metropolitan populations are quite different from those one encounters in a rural environment because of their intensity. Crime is rampant in the poorer sections of the central cities and the poorer suburbs. These sections are unsafe for anyone, strangers and residents alike. Cities must expend considerable resources providing protection in these areas, although their efforts are usually only moderately successful.

While crime is the most obvious problem typical of the big, older city, urban life there generates many others that affect the legal system and its attempt to deliver justice. Life in the big cities is often impersonal. Although residents live in close proximity to each other, they do not know each other very well. Often there is too much mobility to permit the growth of a sense of neighborliness and community. People are also too afraid of each other and each other's problems. The architecture of many large housing projects does not promote socializing among neighbors. Moreover, many of one's daily contacts with other people are with strangers from other parts of the city. Grocery shopping involves only a fleeting encounter with a checkout clerk who is too busy to exchange social pleasantries. Major purchases, like appliances and automobiles, are often made outside the neighborhood; the salesman is a total stranger. Schools in many areas have a high turnover of teachers, which makes close parent-teacher collaboration difficult. Work is often miles away, and there is little opportunity to socialize with one's co-workers.

Thus, many of the contacts that generate disputes are with strangers. This is most evident in automobile accidents resulting in property damage or personal injury. They are the result of a chance encounter, often with a stranger who lives in an entirely different part of the metropolitan area. Disputes arising from such collisions must be settled in an impersonal way, often with the intervention of still another impersonal agent, the insurance company. Another common source of disputes in the large city involves one's relationship with the owner of one's apartment. Often that is a large public organization (the public housing authority). Alternatively, the landlord is represented by another impersonal intervenor, the realty management firm.

In small, stable communities conflicts can be mediated by common acquaintances, and their resolution can be based on an intimate knowledge of the background of each of the disputants and of the dispute itself. Such resolution is rarely possible in the large city. Conflict resolution needs to be bureaucratized and institutionalized to reflect the impersonal character of life in general. That gives a special quality to life in the large city and makes the delivery of justice a much different enterprise than it is in the small town.

In addition, big cities are often melting pots where people with quite different social and cultural traditions must learn to coexist with one another. Much of city politics consists of the struggles by one group to maintain its dominance while other groups seek to find their place in the sun. The legal system reflects these conflicts. Disadvantaged groups who feel excluded from legislative proceedings (because they did not elect representatives) or from administrative agencies (because their followers have not won positions inside the agencies) may take their cause to the courts. The quest for social justice thus intermingles with the search for individual justice. The same courts that determine on one day whether a person should obtain a divorce or a personal-injury compensation may on the next day decide whether schoolchildren should be bused into surrounding neighborhoods or whether the city must provide a higher level of services to neglected neighborhoods.

Furthermore, the concentration of people and economic activity in large cities generates a different mix of disputes than one would expect in a more homogeneous environment. On the one hand, central cities have declined as centers of production and distribution. In most, the downtown business district has fallen victim to the suburban shopping mall. Moreover, as old factories have had to be replaced, firms have usually moved their facilities to the suburbs or relocated in entirely different regions of the country instead of remodeling old facilities. On the other hand, corporate headquarters and financial institutions have remained in the central cities to a much larger extent. Consequently, much of the relatively small-time activity of courts has moved outside the central city while the major conflicts that concern large businesses still center in the downtown areas of the core city. This means that central-city legal institutions play a much more than local role in affairs of the litigants who use them. The courts of New York, Chicago, Los Angeles, Houston, and Washington not only handle the local disputes of the business concerns located there but also resolve the basic national conflicts that happen to be brought to those courts because of the location of corporate and financial headquarters.

Because of the importance of corporate headquarters and the conflicts they must resolve, big-city legal institutions are quite different from those in smaller towns. Big business litigation has led to the concentration of large numbers of attorneys in law firms that specialize in the affairs of corporations. In many big cities, there are almost two separate legal professions—one serving large corporations and one serving the general population. Each makes different demands on courts; each reflects a different set of priorities for the legal system.

Thus, the principal characteristics of the big city affecting the justice system are the diversity of the population and the distribution of economic activity throughout the metropolitan region. The most severe individual problems occur mostly in the central cities. It is also there that the most important economic disputes arise. But much of the economic activity that generates legal conflicts has shifted to the suburbs, and many of these suburbs belong to different court districts than do the central cities.

FRAGMENTATION

The delivery of justice typifies another city problem: it intersects jurisdictional lines in the same crazy-quilt fashion as most governmental services in the United States.

Large segments of the justice system are directly managed by city officials. The most important of these is the police, which is responsible for maintaining order in the city and makes most criminal arrests within a city. Many cities also have municipal courts with their staffs of judges, clerks, and attorneys. Many cities also provide some funding and supervision for legal-assistance services for persons with low incomes who cannot afford private attorneys. Finally, city agencies themselves generate many of the disputes that eventually come to court. Zoning and housing codes are the source of many such disputes, but the collection of city taxes, the purchase of goods and services by city agencies, and the employment of city workers also generate many disputes.

Justice agencies, however, spill over city lines in most instances. Suburbanization has meant the proliferation of police departments in metropolitan areas. In addition, the courts that handle more important cases are usually organized by counties or groups of counties. Thus, a city often shares courtroom facilities with neighboring suburbs. Such sharing has many important consequences for the delivery of justice. Suburban communities contribute to the caseload of the courts. Many of the key officials—especially judges and the prosecutor—are selected within the larger jurisdiction. That cuts two ways. In some instances courts view inner-city cases from the perspective of the comfortable suburbs and their more homogeneous surroundings. The cruelty of inner-city crime and the harshness of ghetto life are judged by the values of the suburbanite. In other instances, where the inner city dominates the metropolitan political system, just the opposite occurs: suburban cases are judged by inner-city values.

The input of cases also crosses the jurisdictional boundaries of the city. City police are not the only police force active in a city and metropolitan area. The county sheriff often has a large police force. In addition, the national government has several police agencies that may be active within a city—for instance, the FBI and agents of narcotics enforcement agencies. Some direct cases to the local courts; others direct cases to the federal district court, which also sits in the city but has jurisdiction over a much larger area.

The structure of city legal institutions consequently responds to complex forces that transcend city boundaries. The quality of justice is not entirely under the control of city officials. They share authority with county, state, and national officials who in turn respond to their own constituencies rather than only to the city. That means that city officials sometimes have grave difficulties meeting perceived problems because they do not control all of the agencies that have responsibility for delivering justice. Of course, that difficulty is not unique to the delivery of justice; it is typical of almost all services the city delivers.

ABSENCE OF ALTERNATIVES

The legal system and courts do not have a monopoly over the resolution of disputes. In most societies, numerous alternatives exist. These range from informal reconciliation to the involvement of nongovernmental mediators or arbitrators. Urban America, however, appears to be relatively poor in these alternative resources. For alternatives to work, people must be connected by informal links that allow them to have confidence in some outside party who might settle their dispute or that might allow them to trust a settlement proposed by the other disputant. As we have already indicated, those conditions do not typically exist in large American cities. The family is usually simply the nuclear family; grandparents, uncles, and aunts usually live elsewhere, often at a distance. The work place seldom provides a setting for making friends because the people who work together do not live together. Workers are also not usually ethnically homogeneous and do not share church or club ties that might bind them together. Finally, many of their transactions are with strangers in bureaucratic settings. Those settings do not lend themselves to informal conflict resolution. When a person fails to pay his monthly bill, the corner grocer might take his word that family sickness prevented prompt payment. A bank or finance company requires formal documentation because they do not know the borrower as a neighbor but only as an impersonal customer.

Consequently, many disputes that presumably should be settled without recourse to formal legal processes cannot be shunted aside to informal procedures. Those procedures either do not exist or do not have sufficient drawing power to win the confidence of those who might use them. The bigger and more impersonal the city grows, the less available these alternatives to the formal legal system become. This means that in big cities, courts must handle many cases that might be conciliated informally in other places. It also means that those persons who cannot afford the formal legal process must often swallow their losses rather than protest them. The result is unequal justice because the courts, as we shall see, exact a toll from those who use them. Those who cannot afford the courts often have no alternatives but to accept a situation that they consider unjust but cannot remedy.

victims
of crime

*f*or many people crime best represents the problem of justice in the city. Crime symbolizes the fear that pervades many Americans' perception of city life. Americans have long had a penchant for viewing their cities as wicked, dangerous places. In addition, in recent years they have blamed the cities for blocking their achievement of the good life—because they must live in fear of crime.

The facts, however, belie that perception. Crime does not threaten the economic or social routines of most people. Crime is largely an isolated phenomenon. Its victims are concentrated in distinctive parts of their cities. The only portion of the popular image supported by the evidence is that crime is at historically high levels. To understand how crime affects city life, we need to examine the level of crime rates, their composition, and their distribution.

level of crime in the united states

Since World War II, crime has exploded in volume in every category and every part of the country. Figure 2.1 shows some of that increase for the years since 1960. It shows the extent to which both violent crimes and property crimes skyrocketed; violent crimes went from 161 to 482 per 100,000 people, and property crimes rose from 1,726 to 4,800.[1] This meant that robberies (where something is taken from the

fig. 2.1
Crime in the United States, 1960–77

Source: Michael R. Gottfredson, Michael J. Hindelang, and Nicolette Parisi, eds., *Sourcebook of Criminal Justice Statistics, 1977* (Washington, D.C.: U.S. Department of Justice, Law Enforcement Assistance Administration, 1978), p. 397; and Federal Bureau of Investigation, *Uniform Crime Reports, 1976–77* (Washington, D.C.: Government Printing Office, 1978).

victim by force) increased almost three and a half times and burglaries (where a house or store is broken into and something stolen) tripled. Most of this increase occurred in America's cities, but small towns and rural areas did not escape it entirely. Although some decrease in crime rates occurred in the late 1970s, these rates now approach those that historians estimate for earlier periods of American history when cities were crowded with new immigrants and the countryside was typified by a frontier culture highlighted by violence.[2]

Twentieth-century Americans fancy that they have advanced beyond that era. They live in a high-technology society that has saved them even from the scourge of war on their own soil. Americans are accustomed to thinking that violence and brutality occur only in foreign lands and on the television set. They are, therefore, especially alarmed to discover that violent crimes have sharply increased. News stories based on FBI reports tell little about who and where the victims are. Used to having violence brought into their homes by television dramas, Americans tend to interpret official reports of rising crime as a personal threat.

Although the crime rate is high, crimes remain rare events and victims are hard to find. That is the experience of the federal government's victimization surveys, which interview thousands of citizens to find enough victims to allow a reliable analysis of crime patterns. For instance, Wesley Skogan, using census materials, found that 99.8 percent of all persons contacted by the Census Bureau had not, in a six-month period, experienced a personal theft, 99.6 percent had not experienced a robbery, 99 percent of America's households had not had their car stolen, 95.5 percent had not been victimized by a burglary, and 86.1 percent had not been victimized by any form of larceny.[3] Except for household burglaries and larcenies, the surveyors found that victims constituted only a tiny portion of the population.

Crime is not the most dangerous component of modern life. To appreciate its threat, we need to compare it to other disasters that confront modern Americans. Table 2.1 provides some of those comparisons. The data in table 2.1 show that it is much more dangerous to expose oneself to cars than it is to leave property untended. Injuries from auto accidents occur about two and a half times more often than robberies. There are four times as many divorces (each of which involves at least two "victims") as there are rapes or purse snatchings. None of the incidents portrayed in table 2.1 are desirable or socially constructive. All reflect some of the disabling pressures of modern urban life, but they show that crime is only one aspect of that existence and possibly not the most dangerous one. However unpleasant life in modern American cities may be, crime is not the sole cause.

composition of crime rates

Crime is generally separated into two categories according to what is harmed. The one category entails crimes of violence where people are injured or killed; they may also lose property as a part of the incident, as in a robbery. The other category includes property crimes where no

table 2.1

Victimization Rates and Selected Other Personal Disasters
per Thousand Population over Twelve Years Old

Traffic accidents	121[a]
Personal larceny without contact	90
Accidental injuries	19
Robberies	7
Heart disease deaths	6.4
Divorce	4.4[b]
Cancer deaths	1.2
Rape	1
Purse snatching	1

[a]Rate based on total population.

[b]Rate based on population over the age of thirteen.

Note: Criminal victimization and traffic accident rates overstate the number of individuals affected because several incidents may occur to a single individual. That is not true of death rates and is unlikely for divorce rates for any particular year.

Sources: For traffic accidents, accidental injuries, divorce, and cancer deaths, U.S. Department of Commerce, *Statistical Abstract of the U.S., 1976* (Washington, D.C.: Government Printing Office, 1977), pp. 65, 66, 68; for victimization rates, U.S. Department of Justice, Law Enforcement Assistance Administration, *Criminal Victimization in the United States 1973,* Report No. SD-NCP-N-4 (Washington, D.C.: Government Printing Office, 1976), p. 68.

person is harmed, but property is unlawfully taken. These are important distinctions because the two kinds of crimes have very different incidences and quite distinct meanings for their victims.

The most common crimes are those involving the theft of property. Property victimizations—whether from a single person or from a household—occur much more often than violent crimes against a person. For every violent crime, there are ten property crimes reported to the police.[4]

It is not easy to estimate what effect these thefts have on their victims or on the economy as a whole. Personal loss is often cushioned by insurance. Much stolen property is insured, and the insurance company compensates the victim. That means that the victim pays for his loss on the installment plan. Potential victims purchase insurance because they know that they run a considerable risk of loss through theft and burglary. They regularly pay the premiums and occasionally collect on claims. Insurance also shifts some of the immediate cost from those who have been victimized to some who are not suffering a loss at the moment.

The personal burden of property crime falls unevenly on the

population. For some, especially the wealthy, a loss through theft may be more psychic than economic. Wealthier persons more often have insurance than the poor. They are also likely to be more thoroughly immersed in the disposable culture that marks much of American life. Indeed, given the pleasure that many people derive from buying and replacing the objects that surround them (witness the myriad of garage sales), the loss of property through theft and burglary is only in part a deprivation; for some people it is an opportunity to buy new things. For family victims of property crimes (as contrasted to business victims) the loss of their feeling of security is perhaps more serious than their monetary loss. They realize that a potentially dangerous stranger has invaded their house and burglarized it. Americans like to speak of their homes as their "castles." Burglaries show how vulnerable those castles are.

Economic loss caused by property crimes is difficult to estimate. Victims try to pass the costs on to others through insurance or by raising the price of their product if they are a business. The thief and burglar, however, now possess the stolen goods, which they generally sell. The goods—for instance, television sets—produce an income for the thief and are used by new owners who purchase them at relatively low prices. Thus, what is stolen is not entirely lost; it is redistributed through an illegal marketplace.

Statistics about crimes of violence generate more fear than reports about property crimes. Lives are at stake or seem to be. The statistics disguise two important characteristics of violent crime, however. Such crimes occur much less frequently than property crimes, and they often involve friends or relatives of the assailant. We have already shown how much lower the violent crime rate is than the property crime rate. In addition, many of the violent crimes take place in the home; some of the most dangerous people we encounter may be our relatives and friends. This is particularly true for homicides and assaults. For instance, in New York City during 1976, only one-fourth of all homicides were committed by strangers; three-fourths were committed by spouses, lovers, friends, and acquaintances.[5] Our information about assaults is flawed precisely because so many assailants know their victims intimately. Many assaults are not reported to the police. Victims often refuse to tell a surveyor about an assault, even if they have reported the incident to the police earlier. The reason for failing to report such crimes is that the victim and assailant often must continue to live and work with each other. Reporting the incident would be too disruptive. Two especially common examples of this kind of assault are those resulting in battered wives and battered children. These have become so common that some cities have established special centers to treat and counsel the victims. Such assaults often come to the attention of authorities not because someone calls the police but because a doctor in a hospital emergency room suspects that a criminal assault has taken place. These kinds of assaults occur much more frequently than official data suggest.[6] Thus, the violent crime rate is higher than most people realize. Much violent crime does not involve strangers, however; it occurs within the family and among "friends." It is the consequence of personal relationships rather than the result of a general social malaise. Nevertheless, enough violent crimes are committed by strangers and they are featured so prominently by the media that they contribute considerably to the image of the city as a dangerous place.

Two conflicting interpretations of the levels and components of crime are possible. On the one hand, we can draw the conventional conclusion that crime has become such a serious problem for Americans that it threatens the fabric of social life. On the other hand, by comparing the incidence of crime with other socially harmful or painful phenomena, we might conclude that crime is only one of many social ills that beset modern urban dwellers. Compared with these other phenomena, crime is not particularly prominent or threatening, especially when one takes into account the replacement of lost goods by insurance payments, the disposable character of many goods, and the incidence of crimes that involve friends and acquaintances rather than strangers.

are all cities equally dangerous?

Most people believe that some cities are safer than others. Official statistics confirm that impression. But the notion that big cities are the most dangerous and that New York and Chicago in particular are the centers of crime is not true.

When we compare suburbs with central cities, we find that suburbs generally have fewer personal and household crimes. That is not universally true for personal thefts, however, as table 2.2 indicates. While robbers and burglars find their victims much more frequently in the central cities than in the suburbs, thieves (see the column for personal theft) work with the same or slightly greater frequency in the suburbs of large cities as in the central cities.

table 2.2

Victimization Rates per 1,000 Population over Twelve Years Old, 1975

		robbery	total crimes of violence	household burglary	personal theft
Nonmetropolitan areas		3	21	65	69
Metropolitan areas					
50,000–249,999	central				
	city	7	41	115	110
	suburbs	3	27	89	97
250,000–499,999	central				
	city	10	45	121	110
	suburbs	14	33	94	104
500,000–999,999	central				
	city	14	50	130	122
	suburbs	6	33	86	109
1,000,000 and over	central				
	city	19	49	96	82
	suburbs	8	38	87	111

Source: U.S. Department of Justice, Law Enforcement Assistance Administration, *Criminal Victimization in the United States: A Comparison of 1974 and 1975 Findings,* Report No. SD-NCP-N-5 (Washington, D.C.: Government Printing Office, 1977), tables 7, 12.

When we compare smaller central metropolitan areas with larger ones, we find that the largest cities are not the most dangerous. Middle-sized central cities in the half million to million population range have more crime victims than cities that are smaller or larger. Thus, cities in the class of Oakland, Oklahoma City, and Omaha are more dangerous than New York, Philadelphia, or Detroit.

These findings are supported by evidence available from victimization surveys conducted in the early 1970s in the five largest American cities and in twenty-one middle-sized cities. The range of victimization in these cities was great, with highs and lows often occuring in unexpected places. For instance, the lowest robbery rates occurred in Dallas and Miami at ten per 1,000 population; the highest was in Detroit at 32 per 1,000. Miami also had the lowest personal theft rate (44 per 1,000); San Diego had the highest (141 per 1,000). New York had the lowest burglary rate (68 per 1,000); Minneapolis had the highest (177 per 1,000).[7]

These are not trivial differences, nor do they confirm popular prejudices about particular cities. New York and Newark do not emerge as the most dangerous places, nor do Minneapolis or Denver appear the safest. There seem to be underlying social forces in these cities that help explain the variations in victimization.[8] Crimes of violence like robbery appear to plague different kinds of cities than do property crimes. Cities with high robbery rates tend to be densely packed and to have declining populations; they are cities with considerable income inequality and residential segregation by race. They tend to have higher percentages of unemployment, foreign-born populations, and blacks. By contrast, cities with high burglary rates tend to be those with smaller black populations, less poverty, more families earning over $15,000 a year, and much lower population density. While robbery rates rise with population size, burglary rates drop with population size. These data suggest that robberies and perhaps other crimes of personal violence occur most frequently in cities that have much social pathology, while burglaries occur most frequently in wealthier, more thriving cities. In geographical terms that means that the older cities of the Northeast suffer more from high robbery rates while the newer cities of the Southwest and West have higher burglary rates.

The crime problem, thus, is most acute in middle-sized cities, and it is more an affliction of central cities than suburbs. Crime is not, however, the same kind of problem for all cities. Residents of older cities of the frostbelt (the Northeast and Midwest) suffer much more from personal crimes of violence. Residents of the newer cities in the sunbelt (the Southwest and West) are more likely to become victims of property crime.

who are the victims?

Crime may claim anyone as its victim. People of every description— old and young, white and black, rich and poor—are among the victims of criminals. FBI reports foster this image of the generalized impact of crime by reporting averages for the country as a whole. The news media strengthen it by emphasizing the human-interest element of crime stories, the bit of "everyman" that characterizes the victims they feature. On an ordinary day, September 12, 1977, for instance, the first section of the *Chicago Tribune* told of a fourteen-year-old boy shooting his brother, of a "series of violent crimes" in San Francisco, about the slayings of "four youngsters" in Michigan, and about the kidnapping and release of a college coed who was the daughter of a small-town banker. The stories tell the age of the victims; one specifies race; only one states their social status. Such stories make it easy for readers to empathize with the victims of crime and to project themselves into their situation, but they give a false impression about the incidence of crime.

Crime does not fall with equal weight on all segments of a city's population. While there are victims in every group, the frequency of victimization and the kinds of crimes that occur vary greatly. The young and blacks are particularly burdened by crime; whites and the elderly are not especially vulnerable.

In almost every city, burglars victimize blacks more frequently than whites.[9] Moreover, because their income is relatively lower and the likelihood of insurance coverage less, the real loss suffered by blacks from burglaries is on the average greater than it is for whites. The same is true for robbery. In most cities robbers attack more black than white victims. The exceptions are Oakland and San Francisco, where whites have higher robbery victimization rates than blacks and other nonwhites.

In most cities, the young are especially vulnerable to robbers. In almost every one of the twenty-six cities surveyed, youth between the ages of twelve and fifteen or sixteen and nineteen have the highest victimization rates of any population group. In Philadelphia, a 1977 study asserted that 46 percent of a random sample of thirteen-year-old black schoolboys were victims of a crime during one year; in the following year, 40 percent of this sample reported being victimized.[10] A similar sample of white boys disclosed 40 percent who were victims of crime.[11]

By contrast, the elderly often have much lower victimization rates. Among a national sample in 1974, for instance, 2.5 percent of the twelve- to sixteen-year olds reported an assault on themselves, while only 0.2% of those over sixty-five reported such an attack. Six-tenths of one percent of the young told of being robbed; only 0.2 percent of the elderly had had such an experience.[12] Moreover, the young and the elderly suffer from different kinds of crimes. In the 1974 national sample, three-fourths of the young victims had suffered from violent crime; only one-fourth had suffered from predatory crimes such as robbery and personal larceny. Among elderly victims the proportions were reversed: three-fourths suffered from predatory crimes and one-fourth had been assaulted or raped.[13] Finally, the location of the incident varies by age. Most of the young are victimized on the street or in school. Indeed, young boys in Philadelphia are particularly fearful of the streets leading to school and the schoolyard itself.[14] The elderly, by contrast, are robbed and assaulted with almost equal frequency in their homes, near their homes, and on the streets.[15]

In part, these different victimization rates among the young and old reflect the residential patterns of age segregation in many cities. Old people do not live in the same neighborhoods as the young. The young go to school, where they encounter a high concentration of juvenile criminals. Elderly people do not congregate in equally dangerous places. Moreover, young people are willing to take risks and are often oblivious to danger, while many elderly live cautiously. The young dare to go anywhere; the elderly stay home in fear. The same is true for many middle-aged persons. The Philadelphia study showed that a considerable number of parents were more fearful than their sons.[16] Almost all the mothers in that study said they tried to avoid danger by staying home at night or going out with someone else rather than alone, by keeping their front door locked at all times, and by keeping their children off the streets after dark.[17]

Both the poor and the rich experience burglaries frequently, while middle-income families are victimized less. In most cities, the victimization rate for burglaries is greatest for the lowest and highest income brackets—under $3,000 per year and over $25,000 per year. In many cities, the rates are highest for the rich but often not significantly so; in some other cities (e.g., Oakland, Houston, Cincinnati, Denver, and Atlanta) the poorest households have significantly higher burglary victimization rates than the richest.[18] Subjectively, the losses suffered by the poor are likely to be greater since they have fewer household possessions and are much less likely to be covered by insurance. The only factor compensating the loss among the very poor is perhaps their greater propensity to buy "steals"—that is, stolen goods at cheap prices.

Middle-income groups suffer less from burglaries than do either of the extremes in most cities. They apparently reside far enough away from burglars to make burglary inconvenient, and they do not live ostentatiously enough to invite incursions from the outside.

These data show that crime does not affect every portion of the population equally. Some groups face much higher risks than others. Poor nonwhites are particularly vulnerable, not only to personal violent crimes like robberies but also to property crimes like burglaries. Young people, especially if they are nonwhite and poor, are among the most frequent victims in most cities. The rest of the population— by far the majority—experiences crime much less frequently. For instance, persons in the thirty-five to forty-nine age group have about half the robbery victimization rate of the twelve to fifteen age group. For the middle-aged, crime is mostly a vicarious experience gleaned from television and newspapers. Burglaries occur with more uniformity across the population, but the burden still falls more heavily on the poor than on others. Middle-income families (earning $10,000–15,000 per year) are the safest; they have only 95 percent of the burglary rate of the very poor and 82 percent of the burglary rate of the very rich in the twenty-six cities studied.

what neighborhoods are affected?

Our knowledge about the impact of crime on different social groups suggests geographical variations within cities. While some crime occurs everywhere, it is concentrated most heavily in a few neighborhoods. Every long-term resident of a city knows which areas are safe and which are dangerous. Boston's infamous Combat Zone, Chicago's west side, and San Francisco's Tenderloin District are examples of this.

Two places are commonly dangerous neighborhoods. One is downtown. Commercial areas often suffer high crime rates because of the availability of loot and the transient nature of their population. Moreover, transportation patterns contribute to crime in commercial areas because these areas are highly accessible from all parts of the city. Criminals can come and go with equal ease. Because thousands of strangers are drawn to these areas, the would-be criminal blends into the crowd and does not attract unusual attention.

The second danger zone in most cities is the slum or ghetto. Here one finds the largest number of idle adults and youths, the largest number of school dropouts lounging in the streets in warm weather, and the greatest density of population. Here much of the criminal population lives, and they typically commit their crimes near home. It is for this reason that nonwhites, the poor, and their young are the most frequent victims of many crimes. They live in the most dangerous areas of the city.

Conversely, most city neighborhoods are relatively safe from crime. That does not mean that crimes never occur. Almost every neighborhood—no matter how "respectable" it seems on the surface—is likely to harbor its quota of juvenile delinquents and thieves, and every neighborhood may be invaded by outside burglars.

But the risk of recorded crime is low in most neighborhoods of most cities. Most neighborhoods are far enough away from the slums and ghettos not to attract criminals. They are stable enough that strangers attract attention and suspicion, making it more dangerous for a robber or burglar to operate.

In one aspect, however, middle-class neighborhoods may appear to be safer than they actually are. Assaults within the family and circle of friends occur in respectable neighborhoods as well as in the slums. In the slums assaults are more often reported to the police because poor families do not have as many private alternatives to turn to. They cannot consult with their own social worker or psychiatrist; they do not call their family physician. Instead, they are more likely to turn up at the hospital emergency room or to call the police. It is not clear that middle-class homes are safer than the homes of the poor if the would-be assailant is a spouse or friend. Such assaults are simply recorded less frequently in middle-class neighborhoods.

effects of victimization

Although all our information points to the concentration of crime in particular neighborhoods and its focused impact on distinct groups of citizens, it is also indisputable that people fear crime whether they have been victims or not.[19] The fear of crime spreads in several ways. It spreads by word of mouth from victims to their friends and acquaintances, especially if the victim suffers injuries in addition to losing money. The second principal carrier of fear is the media. Almost every newscast in big cities features one or more crime stories; every newspaper tells of several each day. Suburban newspapers also display crime stories. These stories easily give the impression that the entire city is unsafe and that everyone must live in constant fear of attack or thievery.

Moreover, crime is not entirely a geographically isolated, racially focused phenomenon. Talk about crime is not the same as spreading rumors about visitors from the moon. Robberies occur in "good" neighborhoods; there are many burglaries in upper-class suburbs. Thus, there is a constant experiential reaffirmation of the fear that is spread secondhand. Although the problem is much less serious in working-class and middle-class neighborhoods than in slums, enough crime occurs to make the entire population consider crime a serious problem.

It is serious enough in the minds of many people that they alter both their private and public lifestyles because of it. A very considerable number of persons, especially in high-crime neighborhoods, are fearful enough to change their patterns of living.[20] Fewer people go out at night; fewer women go out alone. Neighborhood stores close earlier, put up bars across their windows, or hire armed guards. People are afraid to go out for entertainment, to use their parks, to stroll through their streets. People invest in locks and other security equipment, including handguns. In some neighborhoods, families are fearful of leaving their apartment untended and so keep one family member present at all times to ward off burglars. People avoid neighborhoods they feel are unsafe; they attempt to flee to what they perceive to be safer neighborhoods, thus adding to the drain on the central city and the bloat of the suburbs. Few persons engage in all these activities; at most, people engage in only one or two. But these altered behavior patterns have spread broadly through the American population. They typify citizen behavior in "safer" cities as well as in more "dangerous" ones, in "safer" neighborhoods as well as in risky ones. Thus, although the objective incidence of crime is lower than the incidence of many other dangers of modern urban living and although its incidence concentrates more on certain population groups than do dangers like auto accidents or family disintegration (through divorce), its effects are more widespread than either of those in terms of defensive reactions. Those defensive reactions are broadly considered to have lowered the quality of life in American cities. Consequently, in addition to the direct injuries inflicted by violent crimes and the immediate losses that result from property crimes, crime fundamentally affects the ways in which many Americans pursue their lives in American cities.

The crime issue has also infected the public life of most American cities. In one mayoral election after another, the fight against crime has been one of the key issues raised by candidates, and the crime issue has propelled the police chief into the mayor's office of such large cities as Philadelphia and Minneapolis. In one sense, of course, it is not an issue: no mayoral contender favors more crime or doing less about it. Rather, candidates vie for the image of crime buster by pledging more vigorous law enforcement and harsher treatment of offenders. Thus, crime has become a highly visible issue in urban politics.

As we have noted, crime in fact is much more a problem for the poor than for the rich. Because the public does not fully recognize this, it is one of the few poor-people's problems that attract genuine attention from the entire population. It is doubtful that crime would have such a high place on municipal agendas if its incidence were still more concentrated or if fear of crime were not as widespread as it is. No other problem of the ghetto attracts as much attention and widespread support as crime.

Because so many people fear crime, it is on every mayor's agenda. Crime, however, is a difficult problem for municipal officials to deal with, in large part because of the motivations that attract people to violence and theft. To understand why so little is accomplished, we need to learn who criminals are and how they work.

notes

1 U.S. Department of Commerce, *Social Indicators, 1976* (Washington, D.C.: Government Printing Office, 1977), p. 247.

2 Ted R. Gurr, *Rogues, Rebels and Reformers* (Beverly Hills, Calif.: Sage Publications, 1976), pp. 62–63.

3 Wesley G. Skogan, unpublished materials. See also Wesley G. Skogan, "Public Policy and the Fear of Crime in Large American Cities," in *Public Law and Public Policy*, ed. John A. Gardner (New York: Praeger Publishers, 1977), p. 9.

4 Michael R. Gottfredson, Michael J. Hindelang, and Nicolette Parisi, eds., *Sourcebook of Criminal Justice Statistics, 1977* (Washington, D.C.: U.S. Department of Justice, Law Enforcement Assistance Administration, 1978), p.397.

5 *New York Times*, April 20, 1977, p.1.

6 *San Jose Methods Test of Known Crime Victims* (Washington, D.C.: U.S. Department of Justice, 1972); Deidre Gaquin, "Victimization Surveys as a Source of Data in Spouse Abuse" (unpublished paper, 1978).

7 U.S. Department of Justice, *Criminal Victimization Surveys in Eight American Cities*, Report No. SD-NCS-C-5 (Washington, D.C.: Government Printing Office, 1976), table 6; U.S. Department of Justice, *Criminal Victimization Surveys in Thirteen American Cities*, Report No. SD-NCP-C-4 (Washington, D.C.: Government Printing Office, 1975), table 3; U.S. Department of Justice, *Criminal Victimization Surveys in Chicago, Detroit, Los Angeles, New York, and Philadelphia*, Report No. SD-NCS-C-6 (Washington, D.C.: Government Printing Office, 1976), table 5.

8 Barbara Boland, "Patterns of Urban Crime," in *Sample Surveys of the Victims of Crime*, ed. Wesley G. Skogan (Cambridge, Mass.: Ballinger Publishing Co., 1976), p. 36.

9 Ibid., p. 32.

10 Leonard D. Savitz, Michael Lalli, and Lawrence Rosen, *City Life and Delinquency: Victimization, Fear of Crime, and Gang Membership* (Washington, D.C.: National Institute for Juvenile Justice and Delinquency Prevention, 1977), p. 14.

11 Ibid., p. 26.

12 George E. Antunes and others, "Patterns of Personal Crime Against the Elderly," *Gerontologist*, 17 (1977), 324.

13 Ibid.

14 Savitz, Lalli, and Rosen, *City Life*, p. 34.

15 Antunes and others, "Patterns of Personal Crime," p. 324.

16 Savitz, Lalli, and Rosen, *City Life*, p. 24.

17 Ibid., p. 36.

18 U.S. Department of Justice, *Criminal Victimization Surveys in Eight Cities*, tables 8 and 14; U.S. Department of Justice, *Criminal Victimization Surveys in Thirteen American Cities*, tables 3 and 4; U.S. Department of Justice, *Victimization Surveys in Chicago, Detroit, Los Angeles, New York and Philadelphia*, tables 8 and 14.

19 Skogan, "Public Policy and the Fear of Crime," pp. 8–9.

20 James Garofalo, *Public Opinion about Crime: The Attitudes of Victims and Nonvictims in Selected Cities* (Washington, D.C.: U.S. Department of Justice, Law Enforcement Assistance Administration, 1977), pp. 25, 81.

crime
as an urban
occupation

*m*ost criminals live and work in cities for the same reasons that other Americans do: their job opportunities are best in urban areas. Chances to commit crimes abound in the city, and the potential payoff is high. In addition, the conditions thought to be associated with criminality are also found most prominently in cities.

causes of crime

The causes of criminal behavior are many, and they are related to each other in complicated and only partially understood patterns. We need, however, to examine the likely causes as best we can in order to evaluate intelligently city-government policies to combat crime.

To begin, we need to understand what we mean by crime and criminals. Crime is not simply any deviant behavior, because much deviant behavior is deviant only in a particular context and is not commonly designated as criminal. For instance, the housewife who overdraws her bank account when writing a check at the grocery store is rarely considered to have committed a criminal act; she did not intend to defraud. A brawl among players at a professional hockey game is much less likely to be viewed as an assault or disorderly conduct than the same activity on a public street between juvenile gang members. *Criminal activity violates a law and is designated as criminal by some official agent or regarded as such by a sizable element of the public.*[1]

There are two components to this definition. First, the activity must break a law; that means that someone must engage in acts that a legislature has declared illegal. Sometimes the legislature is the city council, but usually it is a state legislature or Congress; city officials simply administer the laws given them by these higher legislative bodies. Second, the acts must be designated as criminal by some authorized public official or by a sizable segment of the public itself. Not all violations of the law are regarded as criminal, as our examples above indicate. As soon as the police make an arrest, the act leading to the arrest is regarded as criminal unless a more authoritative official such as a judge later rescinds that designation. Alternatively, even though the police do not act, a large segment of the public may think of some activities as criminal and treat perpetrators accordingly. For instance, persons engaged in so-called organized crime often have few arrests on their record; they pretend to engage in wholly legitimate business enterprises. Nevertheless, a large segment of the public thinks of these persons as gangsters and treats them accordingly in public discourse.

Consequently, we cannot simply list a number of actions universally considered criminal. Even taking the life of another person may be justified, as in self-defense, and not considered criminal. Behavior is designated as criminal only in particular social circumstances.

Likewise, criminals are not readily categorized. Not all thieves, robbers, or assailants are alike. Some are rich and some are poor; some are impulsive and some are calculating; some come from broken homes and some come from seemingly wholesome families; some are black and some are white.

No simple or single theory will explain the causes of crime. There is little evidence that crime is universally related to biological traits. Criminals do not differ in their physique from ordinary people. They do not have identifiable physical characteristics that might lead us to recognize them easily.[2]

Nor is there any clear evidence consistently linking particular psychological traits with criminal behavior. While some criminals display mental disorders, many persons with the same disorders do not commit criminal acts. Psychiatric diagnosis is usually too inexact to assist us in determining the causes of crime. For instance, the determination that a person is a "psychopath" largely depends on behavior that is criminal in nature. The terms *psychopath* and *criminal* are often used interchangeably. There are no symptoms independent of criminal behavior that reliably separate the criminal from the non-criminal.

More complex explanations of criminal behavior have been put forward by students of juvenile delinquency. Of the many theories about the genesis of delinquent behavior, the most convincing is that proposed by Cloward and Ohlin.[3] They point out that Americans are taught to accept quite demanding goals for personal advancement. Most people expect to be in a better occupation than their fathers and to own expensive stereo equipment, elegant furniture, good clothes, and their own homes. But many Americans have little opportunity to attain those goals. Early in their childhood, they realize that nothing they can do will enable them to fulfill their expectations. The gap between expectations and actual opportunities poses serious problems. People may try to lower their expectations, but that is difficult in the light of the cultural and social pressures impinging on them; it requires admitting personal weakness and failure. Alternatively, they may attribute their failure to society and begin to deny the legitimacy of the social norms that underlie criminal laws. They may explore illegitimate opportunities to achieve success.

Such explorations of illegitimate opportunities are most likely to develop into regular criminal activities when they are shared with peers who are in a similar predicament. The kinds of criminal activities that such persons engage in depend on the opportunities available to them. That is both a matter of the skills these persons have or are able to acquire and of the available targets.

Thus, criminal activity results from a complex combination of social expectations, differential legitimate and illegitimate opportunities, personal adjustments to the gap between expectations and opportunities, and social groupings. More men than women become criminals in part because expectations for success fall more heavily on the shoulders of men; they are likely to feel the frustration of failure more keenly than women, who often have a ready escape in the role of mother and homemaker. The poor become criminals more often than middle-class men because their legitimate opportunities are much more limited. Youths particularly feel these frustrations and are likely to fall into patterns of delinquent behavior, especially when they drift into the company of other youths with similar problems and outlooks.

Large cities particularly promote the social conditions leading to crime. They are the hub of economic activities that make some people very rich while many remain poor. The gap between rich and poor is most striking in urban centers, and the frustration of those who are unable to close the gap is most likely to be acute there. Moreover, big cities concentrate the poor in neighborhoods where they live close together. Those who are frustrated and alienated can readily find others with similar feelings, and they reinforce each other. Unemployment and the inability to make a good start are particularly evident among youths in the big cities. Large cities are also the places where the most recent immigrant groups gather. Members of these groups feel most acutely the frustration of wanting to advance yet being unable to do so.

Cities also abound in opportunities for crime. Much property is left unguarded in large stores and in warehouse districts that are abandoned by people nights and weekends. Cities are impersonal, so that in many areas strangers do not arouse suspicion. Cities are large enough for criminal subcultures to survive, and these subcultures encourage criminality rather than penalize it with informal sanctions. At the same time, in some areas so few people know each other that informal social controls that might otherwise inhibit criminal activity are absent. Cities also have transportation networks that help criminals move about as easily as ordinary citizens. Many downtown areas are well served by mass transit, which makes them easily accessible to criminals and provide ready escape from the scene of a crime.

Thus, both the conditions that trigger criminal activity in some people and the opportunities for crime are plentiful in most cities. In addition, city governments "produce" crime rates by their decisions about which laws they should enforce. The number of drug crimes, for instance, is in part the function of the attention police give to narcotics traffic. If they wish to ignore marijuana sales and use, drug "crimes" will be fewer and less widespread than if the police decide to crack down on pot. If the police decide to ignore what they consider petty thefts and break-ins, property "crime" will occur less than where police meticulously respond to every such incident. We shall examine this element of the crime problem more fully in the following chapter.

characteristics of offenders

Most criminals are found in poor neighborhoods, but they exhibit a wide variety of characteristics despite their common origin. Some of these characteristics stem from the features of the neighborhood culture they live in; others derive from the lifestyles individual offenders have chosen.

Most criminals come from the lower class. They were born into poverty, lived deprived and sometimes neglected childhoods, attended inadequate schools they left before getting a high school diploma, and had few opportunities for upward mobility. Such persons adhere to some of the norms typical of a lower-class subculture.[4] The most important of these traits are an emphasis on manliness and the need for men to demonstrate it, a search for action to alleviate the dreariness that otherwise pervades their lives, and a fatalistic outlook toward life. The first two traits impel lower-class criminals into deviant behavior when legitimate opportunities for "action" do not exist. Unable to support families or even themselves and finding that the more innocent entertainment of middle-class men is beyond their financial reach, these men are more likely to engage in assaultive and wild behavior or drunken brawls that sometimes get them into trouble. These traits also lead some of these men to take implausible risks while committing burglaries, thefts, or robberies. By the same token, the knowledge that they might (and probably will eventually) be caught does not deter them because they feel that they have no control over their fate. Fatalism dulls their caution.

But this overlay of cultural traits disguises many fundamental differences among criminals.[5] One of the most important distinctions lies in their motivation. Some are driven to crime by a desire to attain particular goals; they calculate the benefits and costs of criminal activity and decide that crime pays. They are as rational as the proverbial "economic man"; their behavior is largely instrumental. Such persons are likely to be professionals with a full-time commitment to crime; they are likely to be specialists who engage in a few kinds of crime. They are career criminals whose principal occupation is crime. Such persons concentrate almost entirely on property crimes of various sorts. Some may be safecrackers; others may be burglars; still others may specialize in auto theft or insurance fraud.

Another class of criminals stands in sharp contrast to the professionals. This second group is composed of persons motivated by inner emotional drives that they do not fully understand and cannot control. Such people commit expressive crimes. They assault their wives or girlfriends in a fit of anger; they become involved in barroom brawls because they cannot tolerate insults. They may commit rape in response to uncontrolled sexual drives. Such persons are less likely to be specialists in one particular kind of crime. They may engage in some property crimes as well as crimes of violence, but violence is their hallmark more than stealth. They may be much more ambivalently committed to crime than the criminal motivated by economics. Such persons are likely to have other occupations from which they earn most or all their income. One might almost say that for persons responding to expressive needs, crime is an avocation rather than an occupation.

Persons committing expressive crimes are not the only ones who may be only part-time criminals. Many offenders seeking higher incomes are also part-timers. Only a few appear to be full-time professionals. Large numbers have other occupations that provide them with part of their income; they depend on the fruits of crime only for the discretionary income needed to finance a higher lifestyle than they could otherwise afford. Others are part-timers only because their skills and social contacts are so poor that they do not perceive opportunities to engage more fully in criminal activities.

The two dimensions we have focused on—intensity of commitment to crime and motivation for crime—are related to one another as illustrated in table 3.1. Professionals are full-timers motivated by economic incentives. They believe that they can earn a better living in crime than in the straight world. Part-timers who are also economically motivated are most often lower-class persons whose straight opportunities are limited but who have one foot in the straight world. Juvenile delinquents engaged in serious crime are also likely to be part-timers. There are probably few or no criminals motivated entirely by expressive needs who are full-timers; as the table indicates, those who are motivated by expressive needs are likely to be part-timers. Particularly prominent among them are the square johns, those who are in every way part of the straight world except that their emotions get the better of them and lead them to commit occasional violent crimes.

table 3.1
A Typology of Offenders by Commitment and Motivation

| | motivation | |
commitment	instrumental	expressive
Full-time	PROFESSIONAL	
Part-time	LOWER CLASS MAN	SQUARE JOHNS
	JUVENILE DELINQUENTS	ONE-TIME LOSERS

Source: The labels are adapted from John Irwin, *The Felon* (Englewood Cliffs, N.J.: Prentice-Hall, Inc., 1970).

All types of criminals tend to be young, poor, and male. In 1975, one-quarter of all persons arrested were under eighteen years old,[6] and three-quarters of all persons arrested for serious crimes were under 25.[7] As every observer of American cities knows, crime is a widespread problem among the young, especially among those who are school dropouts and unemployed. Because the unemployment rate among city youths has been two to three times higher than among older workers, the economic incentive to engage in crime has been disproportionately high. In addition, all the lower-class norms mentioned above operate with special intensity among poor youths. They need to prove their recently attained manhood; they yearn for action; they appear fatalistic about being caught. Although crime and juvenile delinquency occur among middle-class and upper-class youths as well, they are much more prevalent among the poor. Criminal courts as well as juvenile courts are the special domain of the youthful poor.

In addition, criminal courts are the turf of the male. Women constituted only 15 percent of all arrests and 20 percent of those for serious offenses.[8] Female involvement in crime has been gradually rising in recent years, but women have not reached parity with men. The major increase in female crime has been property crime, as a larger number of women have entered the labor force and have been exposed to opportunities for theft outside the home. Female involvement in violent crime, however, has remained at quite low levels.[9] At the same time, police are responding to women's liberation sentiments by ending their former discrimination in favor of women. That means that a higher proportion of female offenders are now arrested rather than being handled informally as they were in the past.

Finally, although whites continue to constitute the majority of criminals in the United States, a disproportionate number of the young, poor males arrested for crime are black. For every black who was arrested for a serious crime, there were two whites.[10] The proportion of blacks among arrestees is much higher than their proportion of the general population, however. This statistic lends credence to the widespread belief that crime is principally a black problem. That is far from being the case, but in big cities where there are large black populations, blacks are particularly prominent as defendants in the criminal courts.

Our composite picture of the urban criminal is complex. Criminals are mostly males although sometimes females. They are mostly young, although a disproportionate number of property crimes may be committed by the relatively small number of older criminals. Many crimes are committed by young men expressing uncontrolled emotional drives; this is particularly true of crimes of violence. Rational, calculating, professional, career criminals who make crime their principal occupation are relatively rare; although they may be responsible for a considerable proportion of property crimes, these criminals are driven by instrumental motives. Most criminals are drawn from the culture of the poor and are themselves poor. Many are black. Most live in the ghettos and slums of their cities, and most also find their victims there. Thus, the problem of crime is a particularly acute problem for the city's poor.

crime as occupation and avocation

We may gain a better understanding of the problems cities face in combatting crime by examining more closely the circumstances that produce particular kinds of offenders. Professionals have little in common with square johns; lower-class persons who commit crimes come from still other circumstances. And the breeding ground for most offenders of all kinds—the world of the juvenile delinquent— has still other characteristics.

THE PROFESSIONAL

Professional career criminals are the heavies of the underworld. They exhibit different characteristics than most of the offenders apprehended by the police.[11]

Career, professional criminals are likely to be specialists in one form of property crime. They may be safecrackers, check artists, house burglars, or commercial robbers. Most of these crimes require a modicum of skills, and some, like safecracking, require considerable technical knowledge. Professionals generally concentrate on only one of these crimes, although they may dabble in others from time to time. They depend on the proceeds of crime for their livelihoods; they generally do not hold a straight job.

Professional criminals are closely linked into a social network of other criminals. In part, this is the result of their reliance on the profits of property crime for their livelihoods, which makes them dependent on fences. In part, it is the result of their working with others on jobs. Commercial robberies and safecracking, in particular, require team efforts. Although professionals generally do not work with the same individuals over a long period of time, they rely on a relatively small social network to supply partners for their efforts. Although the team splits up after each job or each small set of jobs, another group forms when money runs low and it is time to pull some additional jobs.

Professionals plan their jobs with considerable care.[12] They have usually developed a number of techniques to decrease the chances of detection. Professionals watch their victims ahead of time in order to maximize their take and to minimize dangerous confrontations. In commercial robberies, for instance, they will find out when the concern has the largest amount of cash on hand and when the fewest number of employees and customers will be around. Entrance and escape routes are carefully laid out. Each member of the team is given a specific assignment. Evasive action is often part of professionals' repertory. For instance, the fence often operates behind the facade of a legitimate retail operation; the burglar pretends that he is selling magazines while ringing doorbells to see whether anyone is home.

Professional criminals generally are graduates from the ranks of juvenile delinquents. It is rare for professionals to get their starts in adulthood; rather, they began as a children to engage in crime and gradually drifted into criminality as a career for lack of any more enticing opportunities. Professional criminals often have little formal education; they lack the credentials and skills required for jobs in the straight world. But a larger than expected proportion of professional criminals come from working- and middle-class backgrounds instead of from the ranks of the very poor. They generally do not share the core values of the very poor. They are more planful and less impulsive; they are not as fatalistic. They reject the norms of the middle class as enacted in laws and social mores. They view the straight world with the eyes of cynics, regarding most straight people as thieves and themselves as honorable.

The professionals are on the whole quite successful in their endeavor. A recent study of forty-nine imprisoned armed robbers (who were losers in the sense that they were arrested, convicted, and imprisoned) indicates that they were arrested once every twenty-eight times they committed a crime as young adults and once every nine times as an adults.[13] When they are caught, they often have the right connections to conduct an effective defense, which will bring a dismissal of charges or probation instead of a trip to the penitentiary. Many of the professionals eventually spend some time in the penitentiary but not until they have committed a large number of crimes and been apprehended a number of times. The sample of forty-nine armed robbers claimed a total of 10,505 crimes. They committed the most crimes as juveniles, and they were least likely to be arrested then. As they grew older, they committed fewer crimes but were arrested and imprisoned more often.[14]

Purveyors of vice also usually belong to the ranks of the professionals. They make a business of providing illicit sex, pornography, gambling, and narcotics to those willing to pay the price. Because they need regular suppliers, these offenders are much more highly organized than the professional burglar; they almost never operate alone. The degree to which they are organized into a regional or national underworld structure is a matter of considerable controversy, but there is little doubt that on the local level they operate in distinct groups. They are also the source of much official corruption in many cities because their operations are especially vulnerable to extortion and because they can carry out their activities much more easily if they bribe police and court officials to look the other way.

Although few professionals are addicts or alcoholics, their financial needs are considerable. One of the reasons they are driven to a life of crime is that they like to live high, partying the whole time between jobs and enjoying expensive women, food, drink, and entertainment. They cannot support that kind of lifestyle from any straight job that they might obtain.

THE LOWER-CLASS MAN

Occasional offenders who come from the lower class also seek material gain from their crimes, but they have neither the skills nor the commitment of the professional. They engage in crimes when opportunities cross their paths and when their needs become acute.[15]

Lower-class occasional offenders are much less likely to specialize in any particular crime. They participate in whatever activities are available and attractive at the moment. Consequently, they have failed to develop the professional's repertory of skills. They are excluded from the crimes that require skills; when they participate on a team, they are likely to be the unskilled laborers, acting as a lookout or as the driver of the getaway car.

Such offenders are also much less planful than professionals. Planning runs against their grain. They lack the long-run perspective of the professional; in addition, they distrust the results of planning—it makes them nervous and unsure. They lack confidence that they can overcome perceived obstacles; they would rather blunder in and hope for success despite whatever countermeasures they might stumble into. As a consequence, these offenders are caught much more frequently than the professionals.

When caught, they often are fatalistic about the outcome of their cases. Instead of planning ahead by saving money for an attorney and making prior contacts with defense lawyers to bail them out quickly, lower-class occasional offenders who are caught depend on whatever resources they have at the moment. Consequently, not only are they more likely to be caught but also they are more likely to be convicted and sent to prison.

These people have a much more tentative commitment to a life of crime than do the professionals, however. They often have a regular job, although it is usually a menial and marginal one. I does not provide them with as much money as they need for the lifestyle they would like to maintain. Like the professionals, they are hedonists and want more money than their jobs provide for fast living. But whether they actually commit crimes depends on the opportunities that cross their paths.

SQUARE JOHNS AND ONE-TIME LOSERS

Many of the offenders the police arrest are not professionals or lower-class occasionals. Rather, they are semipros and amateurs who are derisively known as "one-time losers."[16] They differ from professionals in many ways. They range over the entire spectrum of crime, with many involved in violent crimes as well as property crimes. Most of these offenders are not specialists; they engage in theft one day, burglary the next, and assault on the third. Few of them are involved in crimes that require skill. They are more often motivated by expressive rather than instrumental motives.

One-time losers are more loosely tied into the criminal social network than professionals. They commit many of their crimes alone. When they require assistance, they will pick up a partner almost by chance and with little screening. Their loose association with the social network of criminals is also the result of their lesser dependence on a particular fence; they are less likely to have a permanent connection because they are not regular suppliers.

A one-time loser is much less planful than a professional. Many of the crimes that he commits are carried out on impulse. He sees a car that he wants to ride in, and he steals it; he goes by a house that looks unoccupied, and he burglarizes it; he notices an elderly lady walking alone in the dark, and he snatches her purse. They are very much opportunists. As a consequence, the take from their capers is likely to be much smaller than that of professionals. Like lower-class occasional offenders, one-time losers are likely to hold straight jobs, at least occasionally. They do not depend entirely on the proceeds of crime for their livelihood.

One-time losers are more likely to share the dominant norms of society than are other offenders. They often are not rebels against society; indeed, they see themselves as members of the law-abiding masses and recognize that they have transgressed against reasonable norms. Although society at large often sees them as part of the criminal underworld, they themselves reject that culture.

Drug addicts who engage in crime share many of the characteristics of one-time losers.[17] They are impulsive rather than planful; they commit a wide variety of crimes, responding to their need for funds to buy a fix and to the opportunities to pull off a job. They generally take much greater risks than professionals because of their immediate need for drugs, which cannot be deferred without considerable discomfort and even pain. Because they are opportunists, they often obtain only small amounts of money from their capers and they must commit large numbers of crimes to sustain their habit. They have little time for planning because of the large amount of time they need to make their connection and buy their drugs. Unlike many one-time losers, however, a larger proportion of the addict criminals are of working- and middle-class backgrounds and hold straight jobs in addition to their criminal careers. They also do not reject the norms of the straight world except as they relate to drugs.

JUVENILE DELINQUENTS

Delinquency (which here means juvenile crime) takes many forms. Some is individual behavior by loners or outcasts from the peer group. Much, however, is group or gang behavior. Gangs vary in their focus: some concentrate on property crime, others on inflicting violence, and still others on the use of narcotics.[18]

Gangs that concentrate on property crime are most likely to exist in slum communities that are relatively well integrated and stable. To make theft worthwhile, young criminals need connections with adult offenders and quasi-legitimate fence operations such as pawnshops.

These kinds of gangs enforce their own moral and normative code. Not only do they require some degree of skill from their members but also they tend to frown on unnecessary violence because it endangers other members of the gang. The boys who belong to such gangs range over the entire adolescent age span. As the boys grow older, they either graduate to the adult criminal world (which their gang helps them contact) or they drop out of the criminal world after finding a job. Such gangs appear to respond favorably to intervention by social workers who specialize in street gangs; their striving for success can apparently be reoriented toward legitimate opportunities if they are made available.

Violent gangs are quite different. Their activities seek to demonstrate "heart"; they work hard to protect their turf and "rep." Violent gangs exist more frequently in less integrated slums where there is greater mobility and social disorganization. Such gangs do not need connections with adult criminals; their preference for violent crimes may reflect the absence of opportunities for property crimes.

Finally, youthful drug addicts may represent double losers — youth who have not found legitimate paths to success and who have also failed in illegitimate endeavors. Both gangs that focus on property crimes and those concentrating on violence exclude the drug addict as too dangerous and unreliable. Drug addicts operate much more on their own than either of the other two types of delinquents. Snorting coke or shooting heroin is often a private experience. Addicts need connections to obtain drugs, and they may finance their habits by selling to others. Addicts often engage in other crimes as well to obtain the funds they need. In most cases, however, addicts come from the ranks of delinquents who committed property or violent crimes before they became addicted to drugs. Drug addiction alone does not usually recruit newcomers to criminal careers.

Most delinquents, like adult criminals, come from the hard-core slums of the city. Delinquency is a widespread phenomenon, however; delinquents can be found in every middle-class neighborhood. But middle-class delinquents are much more likely to be social isolates; juvenile gangs rarely form in middle-class areas. Individual, isolated delinquents usually have one foot in the dominant culture; they have not rejected it entirely as gang members have. The isolated delinquents experience more guilt and feel more ambivalence about their criminal role. They are only marginally in the criminal subculture.

Juveniles account for a very large amount of the crime committed in the United States. Of the 10,505 crimes that the forty-nine armed robbers admitted to, 43 percent occurred while they were juveniles.[19] In 1974, persons under eighteen constituted 45 percent of all those arrested for serious crimes.[20] Such arrest data, of course, understate the amount of crime committed by young persons because youngsters are the least likely to be arrested; many of their crimes are petty and the police often handle juveniles with sanctions short of arrest. Moreover, many of those arrested commit only a handful of crimes while the hardened juveniles are likely to escape arrest for a long time. Thus, much of the crime problem in cities arises from youths who escape detection or arrest.

conclusion

Despite the dramatic simplicity of individual criminal acts, the crime problem in American cities has very complex causes. Crime is rooted in the general structure of the society that sets goals for individuals and constrains their ability to meet them. It is based on differential opportunities for success and the gap between the rich and the poor. It is also rooted in individual responses to the frustration caused by these social conditions. Consequently, no simple policies are available to cities to eradicate the conditions that breed crime. Superficial changes—such as improved housing or more intensive patrolling—are not likely to alter these fundamental conditions. Those conditions can only be changed—if at all—by alterations of a national scope.

In addition, crime is not a one-dimensional phenomenon. Not all crimes are the result of rational calculation; impulsive crimes are unlikely to be deterred by increasing penalties. The drunken husband about to kill his wife in a fit of rage does not stop to think about the possibility of facing the electric chair should he succeed. The variety of criminals we have identified must lead to an array of countermeasures. City policies to combat crime must fit the criminal if they are to succeed.

Finally, when we consider in a later chapter the processing of persons accused of criminal acts, we shall need to remember that most crimes are committed by the young. Criminal careers are relatively short, even when not ended by imprisonment. By the age of thirty-five, most persons who commit crimes have stopped altogether or commit very few. The most intensive criminals in the Petersilia study committed an average of one offense every five days as juveniles, one every eight days as young adults, but less than two a month as adults. Armed robbers with less intense commitment to crime committed only an average of nine offenses a year as juveniles, five as young adults, and four as adults.[21] That would suggest that most city policy for controlling crime be directed toward juveniles and young repeat offenders.

Community and political pressures guiding policing respond to more than the apparent causes of crime, however. As we shall see in the next chapter, they produce a quite different pattern of police activities.

---

notes

1 This definition closely parallels the definition of juvenile delinquency by Richard A. Cloward and Lloyd E. Ohlin, *Delinquency and Opportunity* (New York: Free Press, 1960), p. 3.

2 Donald Gibbons, *Society, Crime and Criminal Careers* (Englewood Cliffs, N.J.: Prentice-Hall, Inc., 1968), pp. 126–34.

3 Cloward and Ohlin, *Delinquency and Opportunity.*

4 Walter Miller, "Focal Concerns of Lower-Class Culture," in *Poverty in America,* ed. A. Ferman, Joyce L. Kornbluh, and Alan Haber (Ann Arbor, Mich.: University of Michigan Press, 1965).

5 The following typology emerges from a reading of Carl B. Klockars, *The Professional Fence* (New York: Free Press, 1974); John Irwin, *The Felon* (Englewood Cliffs, N.J.: Prentice-Hall., Inc., 1970); Bruce Jackson, *Outside the Law: A Thief's Primer* (New Brunswick, N.J.: Transaction Books, 1972); Neal Shover, "Burglary as an Occupation" (University of Illinois, Ph.D. dissertation, 1971); Benjamin Karpman, *The Sexual Offender and His Offenses* (New York: Julian Press, Inc., 1954); Paul H. Gebhard and others, *Sex Offenders: An Analysis of Types* (New York: Harper & Row, 1965); John E. Conklin, *Robbery and the Criminal Justice System* (Philadelphia, Pa.: J. P. Lippincott Co., 1972). The typology is very similar to that developed by William J. Chambliss, ed., *Crime and the Legal Process* (New York: McGraw-Hill Book Co., 1969), pp. 368–70.

6 U.S. Department of Commerce, *Statistical Abstract of the United States, 1977* (Washington, D.C.: Government Printing Office, 1978), table 271.

7 Ibid., table 273.

8 Ibid., tables 271, 272.

9 Rita James Simon, *The Contemporary Woman and Crime* (Washington, D.C.: National Institutes for Mental Health, Center for Studies of Crime and Delinquency, 1975), pp. 39–46.

10 *Statistical Abstract, 1977,* table 274.

11 Cf. Irwin, *The Felon,* pp. 8–15; Klockars, *The Professional Fence;* Jackson, *Outside the Law.*

12 See, for instance, William Francis Sutton with Edward Linn, *Where the Money Was* (New York: Viking Press, 1976).

13 Joan Petersilia, Peter W. Greenwood, and Marvin Lavin, *Criminal Careers of Habitual Felons* (Santa Monica, Calif.: Rand Corporation, 1977) p. 18.

14 Ibid., pp. 13–19.

15 Irwin, *The Felon*, pp. 29–32.

16 Ibid., pp. 32–33.

17 Ibid., pp. 15–19.

18 Cloward and Ohlin, *Delinquency and Opportunity.*

19 Petersilia, Greenwood, and Lavin, *Criminal Careers*, p. 18.

20 Michael J. Hindelang and others, *Sourcebook of Criminal Justice Statistics, 1976* (Washington, D.C.: U.S. Department of Justice, Law Enforcement Assistance Administration, 1977), p. 528.

21 Petersilia, Greenwood, and Lavin, *Criminal Careers*, p. 32.

the police

*t*he police represent different things to different people. For some, they are the "thin blue line" that guards the civilized city against underworld barbarians. For others, police represent the avenue toward middle-class respectability through secure jobs. In the old-style politics police constituted a major reservoir of patronage and a source of control over numerous small businesses that helped finance the political machine. For those concerned about political subversion, the police are a major tool in an antisubversive strategy for infiltrating "dangerous" groups and sometimes provoking them into actions that allow official intervention. Others consider the police with a mixture of contempt and fear; they are the enemy. To many citizens the police are simply the cops who keep traffic flowing, who are to be avoided while driving, and who are the voice at the emergency number whenever anything untoward happens.

These multiple images reflect the many roles that police play in city life. They create a set of political forces that complicate policy issues involving the police. While crime fighting and justice may seem to some to be the most important police functions, they take place within the context of all the other functions and images. It is no exaggeration to say that the police operate in a whirlpool of conflicting motivations.

work of the police

In view of most observers, preserving public order is the rationale for having a police force. The police themselves see it as their major task. But the crime-fighting component of that task is the most exciting and satisfying part of their work.[1] In hunting down crooks the police feel they are contributing to the welfare of their community in a tangible way; they are doing something that no one else can do.

Fighting crime, however, is both difficult and frustrating. Most crimes occur out of the view of the police. That is true in part because criminals make certain that the police are not around before they steal something or break into a house or business. But it is also true because most crimes occur in private places where the police rarely intrude unless called. The police know of the crime only because a victim or witness has called them; then they react. Consequently, police rarely interrupt a crime in progress. Rather, they come after it has been completed and usually when the offender has already fled.

Police success in the reactive mode depends on citizen cooperation. If people call while the offense is still taking place, police can respond in time to make an arrest. This is often the case with barroom fights and domestic quarrels. Likewise, when a burglar trips a silent alarm, the police may arrive in time to apprehend him. But most calls come too late.[2] All the police can then do is record the incident and hope to catch the offender another time. Because the police are often unable to catch the offender, many people do not call them after being victimized by a theft or burglary.[3] The only function the police can serve is to record the loss for insurance purposes; if the victim is not insured, he has little reason to call the police. In other instances, the victim may not trust the police and therefore fails to call them. Since the police are not always called, patrolling by itself is an incomplete response to a city's crime problem.

Distrust of the police and failure to call them are substantial problems in many cities. In 1970, for instance, it was clear that suburbanites, small-town dwellers, and rural residents had a much more favorable view of the police than city residents.[4] Moreover, within cities, different groups have different opinions about the police. Blacks almost without exception are more critical and often more hostile to police than white residents. In Milwaukee in 1969, for instance, the opinions of residents of a black neighborhood were compared to those in a white working-class neighborhood and a white middle-class neighborhood. Blacks felt much more often that the police were corrupt, bad, unfair, excitable, dumb, unfriendly, harsh, and tough.[5] The black residents also reported greater dissatisfaction with the police when they called them for help, in an arrest situation, and when a traffic ticket was issued.[6] Thus, people in cities and neighborhoods that have the highest crime rates also distrust police the most. Where the police are most needed, they are least likely to be called.

Distrust, however, is not confined to minority groups. Large numbers of other victims of crime do not call the police. In 1975, in thirteen of the largest cities, personal victimizations such as rape, robbery, and assault were reported to the police only 39 percent of the time. Household victimizations such as burglary and theft were reported on an average of 47 percent of the time.[7] More serious offenses were reported more frequently, with the reporting rates varying little from city to city. This means that more than half the time when a criminal victimization occurred, police were not called. For those crimes for which the police depend on a reactive strategy, the police were often unable to do anything since most victims did not inform the police and the police officially did not know that these unreported crimes occurred.

When the police are called, they do not always classify the incident as criminal or make an arrest. For instance, in a neighborhood fight the police simply may keep order and cool the situation down because it is not clear who is in the wrong or whether a crime has been committed.[8] Even when the police consider the incident criminal, they rarely make an arrest. The consequent attrition is illustrated in figure 4.1. Of 2,077 events people thought to be crimes, only half were brought to the attention of the police. The police considered 29 percent of the original number (and 60 percent of those brought to their attention) to involve a criminal act. They made an arrest in only 6 percent of the original cases and in only 12 percent of the incidents brought to their attention.

The police do not depend on citizen reports alone. Sometimes the police become more aggressive. They may stop and frisk every suspicious person. They may stake out businesses or homes that appear likely prospects for a burglary. They may set up a fencing operation to attract thieves and burglars and collect evidence against them. They may traffic in drugs, solicit prostitutes, and gamble in order to infiltrate those rackets. Such practices are called proactive patrolling; they are much more likely to capture criminals than simply reacting to citizen calls, but the costs to the public and the police may be high.

fig. 4.1
Attrition between Criminal Acts and Police Arrest

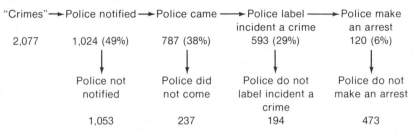

"Crimes"	→ Police notified	→ Police came	→ Police label incident a crime	→ Police make an arrest
2,077	1,024 (49%)	787 (38%)	593 (29%)	120 (6%)
	Police not notified	Police did not come	Police do not label incident a crime	Police do not make an arrest
	1,053	237	194	473

Note: Numbers are number of cases in Ennis's sample. The figure is based on the victim's knowledge; it is less reliable for arrest because the victim does not always know when an arrest has been made in his or her case.

Source: Philip H. Ennis, *Criminal Victimization in the United States,* Field Surveys II, The President's Commission on Law Enforcement and the Administration of Justice (Washington, D.C.: Government Printing Office, 1967), p. 48.

Such aggressive patrolling may enrage a neighborhood where the police appear to harass every young male simply for being on the streets. Such policies apparently contributed to the tensions that eventually erupted in the race riots of the 1960s.[9] At the same time, police involvement in crime sometimes produces crimes where none would have otherwise occurred simply because the police offered opportunity and motive, like drugs. In addition, the risks to the police are very high. They may be discovered and attacked; they may also be corrupted by their involvement in crime.[10]

Proactive patrolling is the only way to combat certain crimes that take place in private locations and in which the victim is an accomplice. The best examples are drug trafficking and gambling. In both instances victims are unlikely to complain to the police because they too have broken the law. Both crimes typically occur out of the view of the police. If the police are to combat them at all, they must use some form of aggressive patrol. For common crimes, however, the evidence is not very convincing that aggressive patrol increases public safety. It may displace criminals from one area to another or from one kind of crime to another. But most crimes continue to occur even in the face of much more police activity in a neighborhood.

It is difficult for the police to direct their crime-fighting activities toward the most likely and dangerous offenders. As we saw in the previous chapter, many of the most violent crimes occur suddenly and without warning in private places. They are often committed by square johns with little or no previous history of criminality. Many property crimes are committed by juveniles, whom the police typically treat more paternalistically than adult offenders. By the time offenders become familiar to the police because of frequent arrests and court appearances, they are often old enough to be tapering off their criminal activities. Consequently, those persons most likely to commit crimes have not usually become special targets for police action.

Indeed, crime fighting accounts for relatively little police time.[11] Because crime fighting is usually reactive, police officers mostly cruise about in their cars waiting for something to happen. They normally see little action because many crimes occur only during the late night and early morning hours. But the police must remain available (even if in reduced numbers) twenty-four hours a day. During the day and early evening, little in the way of crime fighting occurs. Sitting, waiting, and doing things other than fighting crime are the fate of most police officers.[12] It is unusual for ordinary patrol officers to make as much as one arrest a week; it is much more likely that they make less than one arrest a month. Rarely do city police break up large syndicate operations. Domestic violence and petty burglary provide the normal targets for crime fighting by city police.

The police are much more visible, active, and successful in regulating the flow of traffic through the city. They are responsible for enforcing all traffic ordinances. This is important to cities in two ways. First, the smooth flow of traffic is vital to the economic well-being of the city. If people cannot drive to stores or park when they arrive, they will not shop. Likewise, if trucks cannot deliver goods, industry will move to where they can. Second, the enforcement of traffic ordinances provides a considerable income to many cities. The revenue from parking meters and traffic tickets provide many cities with a welcome alternative to raising property taxes.

There are enormous variations in the strictness of traffic enforcement in American cities. One study showed that some cities gave fifty or fewer tickets per 1,000 vehicles; others issued more than 450. In Massachusetts alone, the range was from 12 per 1,000 vehicles in Lynn to 158 per 1,000 in Waltham.[13] These differences are largely the result of the policies and priorities of individual police chiefs. The differences are not the result of public pressure because the public is rarely aware of laxness or strictness and is not organized to pressure the police department. Nor are these differences strongly related to the demographic characteristics of cities or to how their police departments are organized.[14]

Traffic enforcement uses much more of a police officer's time than crime fighting. Departments that have a special traffic division usually have as many patrol officers assigned to traffic as to crime fighting. Where the regular beat patrol officers are also responsible for traffic, that task occupies more of their time than apprehending criminals. It is also more productive. While criminal arrests are rare, traffic tickets are common. Many police departments have an expectation about the number of tickets every patrol officer should write each day; there are no similar quotas for criminal arrests.

The police also constitute the city's emergency force.[15] Sometimes they share this function with the fire department. For instance, one or the other often provides ambulance service. But citizens are likely to call the police, not the fire department, with emergency problems, which range from domestic disputes where violence is threatened but no crime has yet been committed to neighborhood annoyances or disturbances that involve civil disputes more than criminal actions. People also call the police about suspected frauds even though most police departments are not staffed to assess such complaints. Being "Johnny on the spot" means that the police face an enormous variety of tasks. In many instances no clear public policy guides their response. Upon arriving at the scene they must use their own judgment to resolve the situation. Sometimes they refer the complainant to another public agency; sometimes they simply provide a sympathetic ear until the situation is calmed.

Cities have also used the police to protect themselves against real or imagined subversion. During the late nineteenth and early part of the twentieth centuries, the civic elites that dominated city hall used the police to monitor the activities of labor unions, socialists, anarchists, and others they thought threatened their security.[16] In some cases this simply meant attending meetings and reporting the plans of these organizations to their superiors. But often it meant much more than that. It meant infiltrating agents provocateurs into these organizations and using them to promote situations that would justify intervention. In other cases, it meant using the police to break up demonstrations or standing aside while private thugs beat up pickets in front of company buildings. During the Red scare of the McCarthy era in the 1950s and during the peace movement against the Vietnam War, big-city police monitored and infiltrated dozens of organizations such as the American Civil Liberties Union, the National Association for the Advancement of Colored People, and the National Association of Social Workers, purportedly to guard against subversion.[17] On some occasions, the infiltrators proposed illegal acts and helped carry them out; when the police made arrests, they set free the infiltrators who had acted as agents provocateurs and prosecuted the other members of the group. The excuse for such actions was that cities felt threatened by riots—which did sometimes occur—and by the possibility of kidnappings and other violent acts. The police contended that they needed the intelligence gathered by such methods to prevent damaging incidents. There is little evidence, however, that these police activities served any good purpose. Rather, it appears from the files made available so far that an enormous amount of useless information was collected on completely law-abiding organizations and citizens. These operations involved few police officers and little money, but many people felt intimidated by them. They illustrate well the sensitive position of the police in a city's life.

Thus, the work of the police is extremely varied. They have vast responsibilities. Some functions simply require that their presence be known so that potential offenders are deterred and victims can obtain help quickly. Some crime fighting requires aggressive patrol; traffic control also requires active work by the police.

In performing these functions, the police respond to quite different publics or constituencies. Crime fighting appeals to all law-abiding elements of the city, but it plays different roles in the inner city and in middle-class neighborhoods. In middle-class neighborhoods crime fighting plays a largely symbolic, reassuring function. If middle-class people know that the police are around and doing their job, they can be less fearful of losing their property to theft, an event that is fairly uncommon in any case. In poorer, ghetto sections, however, crime fighting has more ambivalent meanings. Such neighborhoods abound with victims, as we have seen; they need and often welcome protection. But the same neighborhoods also have large concentrations of offenders. Many people in these neighborhoods are arrested and many more are harassed on the street because they appear suspicious to cruising patrol officers. It is not always clear to residents of ghetto neighborhoods whether the police are friend or enemy.

The other functions of the police more obviously serve the middle-class and business communities in the city. Traffic flow particularly concerns business people, whose customers, workers, and materials need to move to and from their locations. Of course, ordinary people are also concerned about traffic tie-ups, but what is an inconvenience to them is a disaster for a business. Likewise, business managers are more concerned with domestic tranquility than are ordinary householders because commercial enterprises often have more to lose when riots occur and are more likely targets of civil violence.

The police do not emphasize each of these activities equally in all cities. Rather, they tend to focus on one or another of them so that one can often distinguish between police styles in different cities. James Q. Wilson has singled out three distinct styles that occur in cities.[18] In cities with traditional partisan politics and heterogeneous populations, a watchman style of policing often predominates. In such a city, police emphasize keeping order. The police maintain different standards in different neighborhoods. For instance, they perceive loitering as threatening behavior in one area and arrest culprits, while in another area they tolerate lounging in the street. In such cities the police tend to have minimal entrance requirements and to have unspecialized organization. The opposite police style is legalistic. The police emphasize law enforcement rather than order maintenance. They apply universal standards throughout the city. The legalistic style tends to develop in newer cities with more professionalized municipal services. Such police departments generally recruit better educated rookies; they organize themselves into more specialized units. At the time Wilson wrote, Albany and Newburgh, New York, had watchman style police while Oakland, California, and Highland Park, Illinois, had legalistic departments. A third style is somewhat intermediate between the other two; it emphasizes the delivery of services to citizens. Such departments respond to all calls for service; they do not avoid order maintenance calls (as the legalistic departments tend to), but they enforce the same standards throughout the city. They also have better trained officers than watchman style departments because they find such training necessary to deliver the high quality services their constituents demand. Brighton, Massachusetts, and Nassau County, New York, were examples of service departments.

Which style a police department adopts depends on the character of the city and its politics. The police do not work in a political vacuum. Many groups in the city have a vital concern that the police follow policies favoring their interests rather than others'. The stakes are high in these conflicts, not only in terms of impact on the lives of citizens but also in terms of public moneys and political careers.

people and money for policing

Policing involves many people and much money. In 1975, municipal police departments employed 367,000 full-time persons[19] and spent $5.5 billion.[20] That represented an increase of 12 percent in the number of employees and of 47 percent in expenditures during a five-year period.[21] In terms of per capita expenditures, the amounts are considerable. For the United States as a whole in 1975–76, cities spent more than $44 per person for police protection. Large cities spent the most—$87 per person in cities with a population over 1 million—while small towns of less than 50,000 spent $28 per person.[22] These expenditures constituted about 11 percent of the total municipal budgets in the United States. In large cities, police budgets were a somewhat smaller proportion of the whole budget since large cities spend more on other projects. In small towns where total budgets are smaller, police expenditures loomed larger.

These numbers have extraordinary meaning for some groups in the city. The police have played a special role for upwardly mobile groups in American cities. The police force has always been one of the largest sources of public employment; it constituted a source of steady jobs and an avenue toward respectability among immigrant groups.[23] In the early part of the twentieth century, the Irish as well as some of the other newcomers to the United States found the police a particularly good livelihood. In those days, a position on the force required few skills and little education. These immigrant groups tied themselves closely to the dominant political machines. As a result, tenure on the police depended on electoral success because if the opposing party or faction won city hall, their adherents would get the police jobs. Despite periodic purges related to electoral fortunes, the police remained a source of desirable employment until well after World War I for newcomers to the city.

All that changed after World War II, much to the chagrin of the newest migrants to the cities—blacks and Latinos. By the 1950s most political machines had crumbled and city politics had become much more fluid and more heavily dominated by bureaucratic rules of procedure. Civil-service reform replaced patronage employment and imposed stringent qualifications on police recruits. Recruits had to have a high-school diploma, had to pass a physical examination, and had to be clear of previous brushes with the law. In addition, they were appointed on the basis of test scores rather than recommendations from local politicians. Thus, just as black and Latino groups began to win control over their neighborhood political organizations, the rewards for such control diminished. Employment on the police force was removed from control of the ward bosses and placed in the hands of a merit bureaucracy. Not only did this eliminate any special advantage that blacks and Latinos might have, but it also disqualified many of them because they could not compete on an equal basis with more advantaged groups in the city for police jobs. Most city police forces consequently have fewer blacks and Latinos than one would expect from their proportion of the population, and many fewer than one would expect from the history of the police as a source of upward mobility for recently arrived groups in the city.

These developments add another element to the politics of policing. The demand for employment by minorities is a demand for the same treatment that other groups received earlier. It is a demand that is articulated both in the political arena and in the courts, where minorities have alleged racial discrimination and in several instances won court orders directing police departments to take affirmative action to redress the racial imbalance.

At the same time, police officers on the force have organized themselves to resist the abrogation of bureaucratic rules, which they now see as working in their favor.[24] They do not want an infusion of outsiders or the leapfrogging of minorities over seniority barriers that favor insiders. Considerable racial prejudice exists among many officers, for they come from working-class backgrounds where such prejudice is common and they deal with many unsavory persons of minority backgrounds in their daily work. Accepting minority members into their closely knit clique is especially difficult because their work throws them into extraordinarily close dependence upon one another and isolates them from the rest of the community.

To protect their jobs and to increase their share of the city's budget, organizations of police have developed in many cities. Some of these are outgrowths of benevolent associations that originally functioned to provide pensions, insurance, and death benefits to their members. Now, however, they often seek to represent the police in wage negotiations and to protect against dilution of their benefits and other privileges. In a few cities, the police have joined a labor union to negotiate formal contracts that cover not only wages but also working conditions.[25] Their demands place a heavy burden on city budgets and sometimes bring them into direct conflict with minority groups seeking more police jobs.

organization of police services

The multiplicity of functions demanded of the police, their size, and the political sensitivity of police services make the character of police department organization a crucial one. It determines who controls what the police do and how they are held accountable. It also determines how a large part of any city's budget is spent and what is accomplished.

The police constitute the largest department in all cities that do not also run the public schools. Almost every municipality has its own police department.

Unlike any other municipal agency except the fire department, police are organized along quasi-military lines. They are uniformed and wear the insignia of their rank; lower-ranking patrol officers are expected to salute high-ranking officers. The ranks remind one of the military: patrol officer, sergeant, lieutenant, captain. They stand inspection every day. They are expected to respond to calls for assistance at any time, whether or not they are on duty. They are armed and specially trained in the use of their weapons.

In most cities, the police are organized along two principles.[26] One divides them geographically across the city. In many large cities, police are assigned to geographic precincts; they report to their precinct headquarters every day and go out from there to their beats. In addition, each officer has his or her own beat—a defined geographical area that he or she is responsible for patrolling. Most police officers today patrol in squad cars together with a partner. In emergencies they may be called to help in another beat or precinct, but their principal responsibility is their own beat and precinct. Their main supervisors are also located in the precinct. The second principle of police organization is division according to specialization and skill. Many police departments have separate traffic divisions, vice divisions, detective divisions, and the like. Each of these usually operates out of the central police headquarters and has responsibility for the entire city, although in the largest cities, these special divisions may also be based in the precincts or districts. Police officers working in these divisions are generally not responsible for a beat. They handle all incidents of a particular kind. Burglary detectives investigate burglaries that have been reported to the police; homicide squads investigate all suspicious deaths; vice squads engage in proactive tactics to combat gambling, prostitution, or drug traffic. Membership in these special divisions (except for traffic) gives higher status to a police officer.

The most important characteristic of police work and organization is the enormous amount of discretion that each individual patrol officer or specialized operative enjoys.[27] Police work is beyond the sight of immediate supervisors. Supervisors usually do not know what patrol officers see and how they react. Even when patrol officers are called to the scene of a complaint by their radios, the dispatchers can only bring them there; they must leave officers to their own devices once they have arrived. In practice, this means that police officers (and their partners) decide for themselves when to make an arrest and when to issue just a warning, when to intervene in a dispute and when to stand aside, when to react gently and when to respond with force. Such decisions involve the liberty of suspects and sometimes their lives, but they go largely unsupervised.

That does not mean that the chief of police and lieutenants do not make a vigorous effort to control the actions of their officers, nor does it mean that police actions are unpredictable and irregular. The leaders of every police department strive hard to control the actions of their officers. They do so by imposing on them a period of initial training when they seek to inculcate in recruits the standard policies of the department. Patrol officers usually undergo a probationary period of several months during which a violation of department policies may lead to summary dismissal. Periodic training sessions and instructions at the beginning of each shift also convey department policy to the officers. Every department has a procedure for processing complaints. One value of outsiders' complaints is that they provide supervisors with an opportunity to intervene in the exercise of patrol officers' discretion. But all of these mechanisms do not eliminate the discretion available to patrol officers.

Patrol officers generally use this discretion in regular, predictable ways, however. Every department has its own culture of ongoing norms. These norms have developed over the years as the result of dealing with the city's police problems. They are conveyed to rookies informally during the first months of police work. Rookies learn how to respond to threatening situations by working alongside veterans and picking up their style of operation. Listen, for instance, to one field-training officer speaking to his rookie partner:

> I hope the academy didn't get to you. It's a bunch of bullshit as far as I can tell. . . . Most of those guys they've got working there haven't been on the street for ten years. They can't teach ya nothing 'cause they don't know what it's like anymore. Only a working cop can teach you that the laws and procedures don't translate very easily to the action on the street.[28]

A rookie writing his first traffic ticket comes away from the civilian's car with these observations:

Keith was always telling me to be forceful, to not back down and to never try and explain the law or what we are doing to a civilian. I didn't really know what he was talking about until I tried to tell some kid why we have laws about speeding. Well, the more I tried to tell him about traffic safety, the angrier he got. I was lucky to just get his John Hancock on the citation. When I came back to the patrol car, Keith explained to me just where I'd gone wrong. You really can't talk to those people out there, they just won't listen to reason.[29]

The way civilians respond to police officers' assertions of authority play an important and regular role in determining the ways they exercise their discretion.[30] The more threatening the civilian—whether complainant or the alleged offender—the more likely it is that the police officer will respond with force and by making an arrest rather than issuing a warning or trying to resolve the situation without an arrest. Patrol officers have to learn quickly how to respond to different kinds of people. One patrolman put it this way:

You can't look like a boy scout when you're on the street. You've gotta make them think you'd just as soon blow their head off as talk to them. . . . Not everybody of course, but it's not you're [sic] average creep you've got to worry about. It doesn't take long to figure out who the assholes are out there and they're the ones you gotta put on the I-chew-nails routine for.[31]*

The police officer combines his or her knowledge of the beat, the context of the situation, and demeanor of the person he or she is confronting to determine a response. It is difficult for headquarters to codify that response for the officer, but it follows some regular patterns.

Nevertheless, the leaders of a department have incentives at their disposal to induce patrol officers to follow the broad policy outlines they prefer. Every patrol officer is sensitive to the possibility of being assigned to bad shifts or undesirable beats. None wishes to be delayed in promotions; all would prefer commendations to reprimands in their personnel files. The most serious misbehavior may lead to dismissal from the force and loss of pension rights. That sanction is rarely imposed, but the threat is real.

* These three excerpts from "Working the Street: A Developmental View of Police Behavior" by John Van Maanen are reprinted from *The Potential for Reform of Criminal Justice*, Herbert Jacob, Editor, Volumn III, Sage Criminal Justice System Annuals © 1974, pp. 92–93, 117, by permission of the Publisher, Sage Publications, Inc. (Beverly Hills/London).

Thus, to say that police exercise a great deal of discretion is not to say that they are lawless and unsupervised. They are subject to less supervision than most line personnel in city agencies, but policy makers do constrain the general bounds of their actions.

Control and supervision of police work pose difficult administrative and political problems. Administratively, control is difficult because of the low visibility of much police work. Supervisors must depend to a considerable degree on self-reports. In many instances, the final product is much more difficult to measure for police work than for most municipal services, since what the police are supposed to do is to prevent crime. The number of arrests is not a good measure of such activity because making an arrest depends on much more than alertness and skill by the police. It depends at least as much on their being called to the scene quickly by citizen witnesses or victims. Even traffic ticket production is not always a measure of police work because the opportunity to give tickets depends on the willingness of people to violate traffic laws. If enforcement increases compliance with traffic laws, the productivity of police as measured by traffic tickets will decline even though the police are being successful at their task. Moreover, many important police actions occur completely out of view of supervisors. The ways in which they interact with citizens while patrolling or responding to calls for assistance play a large role in forming the department's image. But these are activities that supervisors can rarely observe directly.

Supervisors may use public complaints or undercover investigators to check inefficiency or wrongdoing, but both alternatives are costly and often ineffective. Police tend to be a very closely knit and self-protective group. Consequently, complaints are often taken lightly and undercover units meet with strong resistance from the force. When outsiders have suggested a civilian police-review board, police officers have mounted vigorous opposition and been able to kill such plans through pressure on elected officials or through referendum campaigns.[32]

Control over the police by elected officials has met with opposition from other quarters. For a long time in American history, city police were extensions of city political machines.[33] Police precinct boundaries usually paralleled city ward lines; that convergence enabled the ward committeeman or alderman to control the police in his area. He hired and fired patrol officers and determined how the law was to be enforced in his district. Police chiefs came and went at the whim of the machine. All that has changed. The political machine has almost disappeared; it has been replaced by the fluid politics of individual candidates for city office and the pressures of local interest groups. An important symbol of the change has been the divorce of police precinct boundaries from ward lines. In most cities, police precincts either have been entirely eliminated or now overlap political boundaries in ways that would make control by aldermen extremely difficult. At the same time, the police have taken on a veneer of professionalism, asserting that their task does not permit political interference. Consequently, the opportunities for asserting political control have diminished greatly. Usually only mayors can try to control the police, and in many cities they do not have the political or administrative clout to assert control. Politically they may be too weak to determine city council decisions, especially in the budgetary process. Administratively, mayors often find that supervision over the police rests with a board they can influence only indirectly. Although titular chief of the city, mayors often find that they cannot direct the police to follow policies the police hierarchy opposes.

Mayors—and, in turn, police chiefs—are also sometimes constrained by patrol-officer organizations or unions.[34] Attempts to alter patrol patterns, to institute one-officer patrol cars, or to establish tighter controls over police discretion have in one city or another led to a clash with the patrol officers' organization. In some instances, the proposed changes had to be abandoned; in others, they were adopted only after considerable public dispute.

Consequently, it is almost a given that control over the police is difficult to establish. As with any large organization, inertia and momentum are the most powerful forces guiding the police. To alter the direction of police services often requires considerable effort. The top brass in the police department have the power to change the direction of police operations even though they cannot control the minutiae of police work. That same power is sometimes denied the political leadership of the city. Control over the police can rarely be taken for granted; it must almost always be actively sought after and asserted.

politics of policing

Disputes about policing may play a central role in city politics or they may be almost invisible. Much depends on the size of the city and the degree to which citizens and officials perceive crime as a pressing problem. In large cities, crime was rated as a severe problem by 80 percent of the population in early 1978; in smaller cities (with less than 250,000 population) 56 percent rated crime as severe; in suburbs only 20 percent rated crime a severe problem.[35] Thus it is not surprising that a study of the predominantly small cities in the San Francisco Bay area revealed that these municipalities did not perceive crime as an important problem even during the height of the law-and-order controversy in 1966 and 1967. All but two of the cities studied were quite small, and even in the two exceptions—Oakland and San Jose —the city council saw other problems as having a higher priority.[36]

Indeed, the politics of policing seems to operate at two levels. The first involves routines that rarely attract attention. City councils find no reason to alter existing ordinances because they already define unlawful behavior with sufficient precision to permit the police to do their work. Mayors need only provide routine support for the police by recommending marginally larger budgets. Policing breaks into the second level of public controversy and attention only in time of crisis—when a riot breaks out, after a series of spectacular crimes or corruption, or when incremental budgetary increases do not satisfy increasing union militancy. At the second level, policing becomes a central issue in city politics and pervades public debate and political campaigns. It more frequently reaches the second level in large cities than in small ones.

Policing becomes controversial in several ways. The most visible issue is whether the police are doing enough to control crime. During the 1970s it was rare for mayoral candidates to fail to promise— among other things—to improve the efficiency and effectiveness of their city's police department. Often that meant promising the department more officers or better equipment. As Skogan has shown, the effectiveness and efficiency of police departments does seem to improve with the commitment of more officers and higher per capita expenditures.[37] The cities that employ more than the average number of officers, provide their police with better than the average equipment, and use computers more than the average police department make more arrests in proportion to the crimes reported to them. They also make more arrests proportionate to the number of police officers they employ.

Police departments, however, have found it difficult to increase their effectiveness by using novel resource-allocation strategies. In a celebrated experiment conducted in 1972 in Kansas City, it was shown that intensive preventive patrolling had no discernible effect on the incidence of crimes known to the police.[38] Thus, the simple expedient of shifting greater resources to the police department did not bring corresponding improvements in public safety. Nor was there a symbolic payoff; the public did not report feeling safer.

Other research by Ostrom and her associates has demonstrated that better training of the police also does not improve the public's image of the police.[39] One of the old bugaboos of delivering municipal services effectively—the fragmentation of service providers across the many jurisdictions in a metropolitan area—does not apparently seriously hinder the police. There is usually sufficient cooperation and collaboration among central-city and suburban police departments to prevent criminals from using municipal boundaries as havens.[40]

The distribution of police within a city also sometimes generates controversy. Some neighborhoods feel neglected and demand more patrols. Evidence from a number of cities, however, seems to show that allocation of police resources flows from bureaucratic rules rather than from the exertion of political influence. Police departments are more likely to increase patrols in response to a neighborhood's crime rate than to its alderman's complaints. That means that poor neighborhoods often get more policing than affluent areas.[41]

The simple presence of police makes a difference on crime. When there are no police, as during a strike, or when they are severely handicapped, as during a total electrical blackout, crime appears to rise dramatically.[42] Thus, one cannot say that the police have no impact. But within the relatively narrow range of variation available to city governments to reduce or increase the number of police officers or their equipment, only small changes in effectiveness can be discovered. While candidates for office may promise much better performance, they can rarely deliver it. The promises may easily lead to unjustified expectations among the electorate and to cynicism about the subsequent delivery of better protection through lowered crime rates.

The police also frequently figure in other political controversies. They are often charged with corruption; they are often accused of racial discrimination; they are increasingly organized into unions, which seek to improve their wages and working conditions through collective bargaining.

Corruption is an endemic problem for the police. Their close contact with criminals, the many temptations presented to them, and the closed world they live in increase the probability of corruption.[43] It may begin with an apparently innocent act such as accepting gratuities from merchants in exchange for keeping a closer eye on their establishments. Sometimes it leads to such serious acts as the systematic milking of regulated businesses like bars and theaters for weekly payoffs in return for "protection." Large-scale prosecutions for that kind of corruption rocked the New York City and Chicago police departments in the mid-1970s and occurred to a lesser degree in many other cities. The temptations leading to corruption are described well by Jonathan Rubinstein in writing of the police officer and vice work:

> The patrolman is obliged to violate the law, degrade people, lie, and even shame himself in his own eyes in order to make arrests he knows are meaningless and he suspects produce money for others. . . . He sees himself as a special kind of fool. He sees himself operating in a world where "notes" are constantly floating about, and only the stupid, the naive, and the fainthearted are unwilling to allow some of them to stick to their fingers. Even in the most carefully regulated system the patrolman's opportunities to break the law are considerable.[44]

Demands for eliminating corruption are familiar in city elections. Incumbents point to the progress they have made, and challengers insist that much more could still be done. They both are right and wrong. Typically, some actions have been taken to rid the police of the worst examples of corruption, but still more corruption remains in most departments. It is difficult to eradicate corruption in police departments given the work patrol officers do and the temptations they face.

Charges of racial discrimination are also prominent in cities with considerable minority populations. At times, the tension between minority communities and the police has reached the riot-precipitating level. As we have already seen, the police in most cities do not have the same proportion of black and Latino officers as the population as a whole. In addition, many of the persons arrested are members of minority populations. For the United States as a whole, the available evidence suggests that minorities are sometimes arrested in disproportionate numbers and sometimes in almost the exact proportion to the crimes they appear to commit. As table 4.1 shows, victims perceive their assailants to be members of minorities less often in rape cases than the persons police arrest, but in assaults and robberies this bias does not exist. We do not know why such a difference exists between rape and other violent crimes. In cases of assault and robbery, as in rapes, the police depend on victim reports. If there is a bias

table 4.1
Victim Perceptions of Assailants and Race of Arrestees
for Selected Offenses, 1975

| | percent black and other minority | |
	victim perceptions	arrestees
Rape	34.2	47.7
Aggravated assault	49.4	41.8
Robbery	61.5	60.5

Source: Michael J. Hindelang and others, Sourcebook of Criminal Justice Statistics, 1976 (Washington, D.C.: Department of Justice, Law Enforcement Assistance Administration, 1977), pp. 341, 488. Victim perceptions come from the National Crime Survey; arrest data come from the Uniform Crime Reports.

against minorities, it lies as much with victims as it does with the police. In assessing that possibility, one also needs to remember that many of the victims who say their assailants are minority members are themselves members of such groups. Thus, the appearance of racial discrimination in arrests may not have a factual basis. But many articulate minority members believe that there is such discrimination, and their belief is reinforced by the relative absence of minority members in the police force.

Unions have become a powerful force in some city police departments. Some departments are organized into local unions, which are unaffiliated with larger labor organizations. Others are attached to the Teamster's Union or to one of the other national organizations. Police unions have often sought a role in local elections to assure themselves a favorable reception when bargaining for a new contract. In cities like New York the police union is reputed to be a potent force in local elections along with other unionized municipal employees. At the same time, because police salaries are such a large portion of a city's budget, these activities and the salary demands made annually by police unions are powerful issues in local election campaigns. Police demands and the tactics they are willing to employ to achieve them (including going en masse on sick call with the "blue flu") are factors that local politicians take seriously.

conclusion

The most vigorous critics of city police question whether police are part of the crime problem rather than part of the crime solution. They are both. Police provide protective services for much of the popula-

66

tion; they arrest many criminals. In addition, they provide many other essential services to the city in meeting unexpected emergencies and in regulating the flow of traffic. In their crime control function, the police exercise a high degree of discretion and contribute to the crime problem in the sense of defining what crime is. Because police are more used to dealing with street crime than white-collar crime, official statistics about crime reflect a greater lower-class bias than would otherwise be the case. By condoning certain kinds of violations of law and crime in certain areas, the police contribute to the crime problem. In addition, police corruption contributes to that problem in a more direct way.

Controlling the police is both a difficult and vital task for city leaders. If they can avoid crises, a city's political leaders can deliver police services with minimal disruption to their routines by providing only marginal budgetary increases and rare statutory innovations. Often, however, city officials cannot prevent crime from becoming a public issue. Particularly in large cities where crimes occur with great frequency and where racial tensions readily escalate into major disturbances, crime easily becomes a political issue. Such cities are also more likely to have watchman style departments than the legalistic or service style departments of smaller cities.

Police can have only a limited effect on crime, however. We have seen in earlier chapters how crime is concentrated among certain segments of the population. In this chapter we have seen how the police depend on the populace to find out when criminal acts have occurred. The persons who could most help the police in combating crime, however, live in neighborhoods where distrust of the police runs especially high. In addition, our earlier chapters showed that many crimes are committed in the heat of passion and could not be prevented by more effective policing. Even criminals who act in a calculating manner are unlikely to be deterred by police action alone. To be effective, arrests require supportive action by the courts and prisons. As we shall see in later chapters, there are many reasons why such support is often withheld.

---

notes

1 Jonathan Rubinstein, *City Police* (New York: Farrar, Straus and Giroux, 1973), especially pp. 339–68.

2 William Bieck, "Response Time Analysis Report" (unpublished report, Kansas City Response Time Analysis Project, 1978).

3 James Garofalo, *The Police and Public Opinion: An Analysis of Victimization and Attitude Data from 13 American Cities* (Washington, D.C.: U.S. Department of Justice, Law Enforcement Assistance Administration, 1977), pp. 30–32.

4 Michael J. Hindelang, *Public Opinion Regarding Crime, Criminal Justice and Related Topics* (Washington, D.C.: U.S. Department of Justice, Law Enforcement Assistance Administration, 1975), p. 10.

5 Herbert Jacob, "Black and White Perceptions of Justice in the City," *Law and Society Review,* 6 (1971), 73; for other cities, see Garofalo, *Police and Public Opinion,* pp. 24–26.

6 Jacob, "Black and White Perceptions," p. 76.

7 Michael J. Hindelang and others, *Sourcebook of Criminal Justice Statistics, 1976* (Washington, D.C.: U.S. Department of Justice, Law Enforcement Assistance Administration, 1977), pp. 404–5. Percentages in text are the median of the mean rate per category for thirteen cities.

8 Cf. James Q. Wilson, *Varieties of Police Behavior* (Cambridge, Mass.: Harvard University Press, 1968), especially pp. 140–71; Donald J. Black, "Production of Crime Rates," *American Sociological Review,* 35 (1970), 740–47.

9 *Report of the National Advisory Commission on Civil Disorders* (New York: Bantam Books, 1968), pp. 6, 144, 299–307.

10 Rubinstein, *City Police,* pp. 372–433.

11 Egon Bittner, "Florence Nightingale in Pursuit of Willie Sutton: A Theory of Police," *The Potential for Reform of Criminal Justice,* ed. Herbert Jacob (Beverly Hills, Calif.: Sage Publications, 1974), pp. 24–27.

12 Rubinstein, *City Police,* pp. 66–68.

13 John A. Gardiner, *Traffic and the Police* (Cambridge, Mass.: Harvard University Press, 1969), pp. 7, 11.

14 Ibid., pp. 111–65.

15 Bittner, "A Theory of Police," pp. 34–36.

16 Robert M. Fogelson, *Big-City Police* (Cambridge, Mass.: Harvard University Press, 1977), especially pp. 13–66.

17 *Chicago Tribune,* Feburary 26, 1978, sec. 1, p. 40; *Chicago Tribune* April 24, 1978, sec. 1, p. 2.

18 Wilson, *Varieties of Police Behavior,* pp. 83–277.

19 U.S. Department of Justice, Law Enforcement Assistance Administration, and U.S. Bureau of the Census, *Expenditure and Employment Data for the Criminal Justice System, 1975* (Washington, D.C.: Government Printing Office, 1977), p. 46.

20 Ibid., p. 26.

21 Law Enforcement Assistance Administration and U.S. Bureau of the Census, *Trends in Expenditure and Employment Data for the Criminal Justice System, 1971– 1975* (Washington, D.C.: Government Printing Office, 1977), p. 24.

22 U.S. Bureau of the Census, *City Government Finances in 1975–1976* (Washington, D.C.: Government Printing Office, 1977), p. 8.

23 Fogelson, *Big-City Police,* especially pp. 13–39.

24 Ibid., pp. 243–95.

25 William H. Hewitt, Sr., "Current Issues in Police Collective Bargaining," *The*

Future of Policing, ed. Alvin W. Cohn (Beverly Hills, Calif.: Sage Publications, 1978), pp. 207–23.

26 George F. Cole, *The American System of Criminal Justice* (North Scituate, Mass.: Duxbury Press, 1975), pp. 203–5.

27 Rubinstein, *City Police*, pp. 339–71; Wilson, *Varieties of Police Behavior*, pp. 83–139; John Van Maanen, "Working the Street: A Developmental View of Police Behavior," in *The Potential for Reform*, ed. Jacob, pp. 83–130.

28 Van Maanen, "Working the Street," p. 92.

29 Ibid., pp. 92–93.

30 Black, "Production of Crime Rates," pp. 740–47.

31 Van Maanen, "Working the Street," p. 117.

32 Cole, *American System of Criminal Justice*, p. 220; Arthur Niederhoffer, "Civilian Review Boards," in *Black Politics*, ed. Edward S. Greenberg, Neal Milner, and David Jolan (New York: Holt, Rinehart and Winston, 1971), pp. 244–49.

33 Fogelson, *Big-City Police*, pp. 13–39.

34 Ibid., pp. 193–218; Hewitt, "Current Issues," pp. 207–23.

35 *A Survey of Citizen Views and Concerns About Urban Life*, Final Report, Part I, Study No. P2795 (Washington, D.C.: Department of Housing and Urban Development, February 1978), p. 47.

36 Heinz Eulau and Kenneth Prewitt, *Labyrinths of Democracy: Adaptations, Linkages, Representation and Policies in Urban Politics* (Indianapolis, Ind.: The Bobbs Merrill Co. Inc., 1973), pp. 525–26.

37 Wesley G. Skogan, "Efficiency and Effectiveness in Big-City Police Departments," *Public Administration Review*, 36 (1976), 278–86.

38 George L. Kelling and others, *The Kansas City Preventive Patrol Experiment: A Summary Report* (Washington, D.C.: Police Foundation, 1974).

39. Dennis C. Smith and Elinor Ostrom, "The Effects of Training and Education on Police Attitudes and Performance: A Preliminary Analysis," in *The Potential for Reform*," ed. Jacob., pp. 45–81.

40 Elinor Ostrom, Roger B. Parks, and Gordon P. Whitaker, *Policing Metropolitan America* (Washington, D.C.: Government Printing Office, 1977).

41 Robert L. Lineberry, *Equality and Urban Politics* (Beverly Hills, Calif.: Sage Publications, 1977), pp. 183–41.

42 *New York Times*, July 14, 1977, p. 1.

43 Rubinstein, *City Police*, pp. 372–433; Fogelson, *Big-City Police*, pp. 32–33.

44 Jonathan Rubinstein, *City Police* (New York: Farrar, Straus & Giroux, 1973), p. 401. Copyright © 1973 by Jonathan Rubinstein.

crime
and urban
courts

*C*itizens may complain, the police may arrest, but only the courts have authority in the United States to punish. Courts must decide whether persons arrested by the police are guilty and what punishment they should suffer if they are.

Courts operate more mysteriously than the police and are even less well understood. Many people believe quite falsely that urban courts face an unprecedented crush of business and that because of the congestion in courts, plea bargaining has replaced trial by jury. Others believe, equally falsely, that criminal courts systematically discriminate against the poor and minorities. Many people are confused about the fundamental tension between the desire for an independent judiciary and a court system responsive to public needs. To unravel these mysteries, we need to examine urban courts as closely as we did the police.

structure of urban courts

American cities employ a great variety of courts. The variation is related to the size of the city. Large cities have large, highly specialized courts. Smaller cities tend to have smaller courts and to share them with the surrounding countryside. In large cities, judges work exclusively in the city. In smaller cities, they are more likely to ride circuit in neighboring counties.[1]

Courts operating in cities are usually called state courts because they are governed by state law; no city can create its own court system. Nevertheless, they are anchored in local politics and tradition and they are often closely linked to urban politics. That is less true— but not entirely false—of federal district courts, which exist in most large cities. These district courts are authorized by Congress but are also closely linked to the local political and legal culture. Except for the informal connections that arise from common problems and a common bar practicing before both local and federal courts, however, no official links exist between them. They operate completely independently of each other.

The number of separate courts or divisions of courts depends on the size of the city and the way a particular state has organized its courts. In some states, each larger city that is also the county seat has several independent courts: one for criminal matters, another for civil disputes, a third for probating estates, and one or two more for other specialized matters. Other cities combine all these functions into a single court but then establish separate courtrooms that specialize in these functions under the supervision of an administrative judge. Larger cities subdivide the criminal courts between those handling minor (misdemeanor) charges and preliminary matters for serious, felony charges and those holding felony trials. Still other courts hear charges against juveniles.

No city has a chief judge in charge of all the courts, both state and federal, located within its boundaries. Very few have chief judges with effective authority to supervise all the local courts. Rather, many of these courts operate with a high degree of autonomy and independence.

When court business grows and additional courts or new judicial structures are required, city interests must go to the state legislature or to Congress with their request. Although urban courts make many decisions affecting city life, lawmakers from all over the state or nation decide on court structure and organization.

staffing of courtrooms

To understand how the courts work, we need to examine them at their operating level, the individual courtroom. Each courtroom contains a separate organization, which we may call the courtroom workgroup.[2] The workgroup is composed of a judge, prosecutors, defense counsel, and clerical personnel. Sometimes these courtroom workgroups are quite permanent and cohesive; in other instances, they are ephemeral, lasting only a few hours, days, or weeks. The degree to which court-room workgroups have permanence is very important to their style of operation, as we shall see later. First, however, we need to understand the personnel who work in the courtroom workgroups.

JUDGES

Judges are the chief personnel of the courtroom. They have the author-ity to run the courtroom. While their authority is not unlimited, it is broad and all others in the courtroom must respect them. Judges make the ultimate decisions and bear official responsibility for them.

Almost all judges are lawyers. Almost all become judges in mid-career. They did not learn judging in law school. Rather, they were practicing lawyers of one sort or another and in their forties or fifties came to the bench. Most judges of city courts come from local, mid-dle-ranking law schools and middle-ranking careers. Few go to the bench from the largest law firms; few were top-ranking students in national law schools.[3]

Judges are selected in a variety of ways.[4] Some are elected in partisan elections, and others are elected in the same kind of nonpar-tisan elections that typify much municipal politics. A few are selected by the state legislature; others are appointed by the governor under a "merit" system where the governor must choose from a list of three or five nominees selected by a commission dominated by members of the bar. In some states the governor makes the appointment without such a screening commission, and in many states he or she makes interim appointments when a vacancy occurs. Sometimes that means that the governor is the principal selector of judges because local custom dic-tates that a judge whose term is about to expire resign in order to allow the governor to circumvent the election system by appointing the successor. This often occurs when the election system is nonparti-san. For instance, a recent study showed that in Minnesota (a nonpar-tisan state) only 7 percent of the judges were actually elected to their first judicial office. The highest election rate for a nonpartisan state was Michigan, with 65.7 percent. By contrast, in partisan-election states, as many as 94.1 percent of all sitting judges (in Arkansas) reached office initially by election; the smallest proportion was in North Carolina, with 31.8 percent.[5]

All of these selection systems link judges to other elements of the political arena. All do not equally select persons who have had direct recent political experience, however. The importance of experience seems to depend in part on the selection system (electoral or appointive) and local customs. For instance, when Florida switched from partisan to nonpartisan elections, the proportion of judges coming from private practice rose sharply, but did not reach the level of Missouri, which has a partisan election plan for selecting many judges. Those Missouri judges selected under a merit plan came almost exclusively from private practice.[6] The data clearly indicate that partisan elections often favor persons who have been in the public eye through other public positions immediately before they seek a judgeship. Ethnic and community organizations have more influence in partisan elections; bar associations have a greater voice in nonpartisan elections and merit selection plans.[7] Many of the judges selected by all plans have had experience in public office in earlier years, however; their private practice was often only a brief interlude. For only a minority is the judgeship their first public position.

City judges' ties with local politicians vary greatly from place to place. In Chicago judges often have had close ties with the dominant faction. When Richard Daley was the mayor, judges usually had close connections with aldermen, committeemen, or other affiliates of the machine, except for a sprinkling of notables who were slated to provide some blue-ribbon aura for the judicial ticket.[8] In New York, judicial candidates needed political endorsement and a considerable campaign chest that had to be contributed to the party to insure slating.[9] Pittsburgh judges also were closely connected to local politics and usually came directly from holding political office.[10] By contrast, Minneapolis judges generally did not have close connections to local politics.[11] California judges seem to require better connections with the governor than with their mayor, and the same appears to be the case in Wisconsin.[12]

Most judges reach the bench at midlife and stay there for the remainder of their careers. Their long careers mean there is less turnover in judgeships than in other courtroom positions. This is true regardless of the selection system. Very few judges lose reelection campaigns; where appointment is the method of selection, most are reappointed. Moreover, judicial terms tend to be longer than the terms for other offices, ranging from four to ten years for state judges and life for federal district judges.[13]

Judges are the least specialized members of the courtroom workgroup. In a few cities (for instance, New York and Detroit) they specialize in criminal or civil matters. But in most cities judges serve on unified courts. They are assigned for relatively brief periods to criminal courts and then are shifted to one of the many civil courtrooms. They may serve on the criminal bench for as little as six months or as long as several years, but it is rare for them to become permanent fixtures in the courtroom. In many locales, judges have less experience with criminal cases than the prosecutors or defense attorneys who work with them.

PROSECUTORS

Prosecutors are responsible for representing the state in all criminal matters. They typically decide whether to press charges and whether to seek a guilty plea. Because they handle only criminal cases, they quickly become very expert.

The work environment of prosecutors varies greatly with the size of the city they work in. If they serve a large jurisdiction, they usually operate in a sizable office with many other prosecutors.[14] If they are in a small jurisdiction, they work alone or with just a handful of assistants. In small cities they often mix private practice with public office.

The chief prosecutor for each jurisdiction—variously called state's attorney or district attorney—is usually an elected official who serves for a term that generally runs four years. District attorneys may seek reelection and often do, but most do not make a career of the office. They serve for a term or two and then move on to private practice or to the bench. In small towns, prosecutors tend to be young lawyers who have been out of law school for five or ten years but who have not yet really established themselves in the legal community. In large cities, the position is coveted and usually goes to attorneys in their late forties. The position is often a key political plum because it controls other jobs and brings considerable notoriety to its incumbent. It is frequently seen as a steppingstone to higher public office.[15] Even though prosecutors are elected officials, however, they do not necessarily respond to momentary public opinion. Believing that the job is a complex legal one, prosecutors act more as trustees, letting themselves be guided by their own ideas of justice, than as delegates bound by precise instructions from their constituencies. Even in a smaller city the prosecutor may view the public as misinformed.[16]

In cities with federal courts, two sorts of prosecutor work side by side and independently of each other. One works in the state courts and is the elected official we have just described. The other operates in the federal courts. He or she is appointed by the president for a four-year term. The office is regarded as a patronage appointment, and every new administration appoints its own set of United States attorneys. They operate under the supervision of the United States Department of Justice in Washington, D.C., although day-to-day matters are handled locally with little intervention by the Justice Department.[17]

The chief prosecutor—the district attorney or the United States attorney—rarely appears in courtrooms except in small towns. Assistants handle most courtroom work. They are young attorneys, often just out of law school, who use the job to obtain trial experience. In most cities appointment to the prosecutor's office involves a mixture of merit and patronage.[18] All prosecutors must be lawyers; the better their professional recommendations, the more likely they are to win an appointment. But in many cities, endorsements from political figures also help. In general, Democratic incumbents appoint Democrats and Republican incumbents appoint Republicans. At one time these patronage appointees, like others, took time off during campaigns to work for their party's slate; this happens rarely today. The general inclination and policy drift of the office are, however, marked by the political preferences of the chief prosecutor.

Assistant prosecutors rarely make a career in the office. Most stay fewer than five years and move on to private practice.[19] Many specialize in criminal law; some assume a general law practice; a few move directly to the bench. In most cities, turnover is high although many of those who leave the office often do not leave the criminal courtroom entirely. They simply move on to become defense attorneys. Generally the ambition of assistant prosecutors lies more strongly toward private practice than political office. They are attuned more to the implications of their work for their private ambitions than to the personal political repercussions that might develop.

Assistants work in one of two modes. Many cities use a zone system in which prosecutors are assigned to a particular courtroom and handle all the cases that come there. If the courtroom specializes in a particular kind of case, the prosecutors also specialize, but if the courtroom handles a variety of criminal cases, the prosecutor must also deal with all of them. Often this means that prosecutors work with only one segment of the court process. One prosecutor, for instance, will take care of the arraignment; another handles the preliminary hearing; a third takes the case to trial. The second mode is called the man-to-man system; it links the prosecutor to a particular case from beginning to end. Whatever courtroom a case is assigned to, the prosecutor follows it. One prosecutor takes care of all stages of the criminal process from arraignment to final disposition. Under this system, prosecutors may specialize in particular kinds of cases—for instance, handling only homicides or narcotics offenses. Even under a man-to-man assignment system, however, prosecutors often handle a wide range of cases because they are simply assigned the next case that comes into the office.

DEFENSE ATTORNEYS

Defense attorneys come to the courtroom from a variety of circumstances.[20] Most defendants are represented by a public defender where such an office exists. Where it does not, indigent defendants are assigned a lawyer from among the private attorneys who practice in that jurisdiction. Some private attorneys specialize in criminal law. Rarely do these specialists handle criminal matters exclusively, but their practices usually entail a considerable number of criminal cases.

The private defense bar usually ranks low in the status hierarchy of lawyers.[21] This is most evident in large cities. In small cities attorneys are less specialized, and less stigma attaches to defending alleged criminals.[22] Many defense lawyers formerly worked for the prosecutor's office. Such experience is important for them because it not only gives them knowledge of courtroom practices but also provides them contacts through which they can informally negotiate cases. It also informs them about the predilections of particular prosecutors and judges and allows them to decide more realistically between negotiating and going to trial. Most defense lawyers work as solo practitioners or in small partnerships where they typically share an office, a secretary, and perhaps one junior lawyer who makes appearances for them when they need to be in another courtroom at the same time. Few defense lawyers work in large firms or have the trappings of the Wall Street attorney.

One important exception is the defense lawyer who works as a public defender. Such an attorney usually works in a middle- to large-size firm environment, although without the perquisites of the Wall Street lawyer. Most large cities now have public defender's offices.[23] The chief defender is usually appointed, but in a few places he or she is elected. The assistants are appointed in the same manner as assistant prosecutors, although political connections usually have less significance.[24] Like their counterparts in the prosecutor's office, assistant defenders are generally young attorneys who want trial experience.

They stay in the job for two or three years and then move on to private practice, although a few move to the other side and join the prosecutor's office for an additional apprenticeship. Like the assistant prosecutors, they may work in a zone or a man-to-man system. But the implications of the zone may be more important to them than to the prosecutor since the zone makes it impossible to develop a close relationship to the client before the trial. Many defendants feel that public defenders do not care about them and are incompetent to deal with their cases, since each time they come to a different courtroom, a new defender purports to represent them.[25] Under these circumstances, public defenders and their clients have little opportunity to build rapport.

Of the three major participants in the criminal courtroom, defense attorneys have the least well developed ties to the city's political arena. The public defender's office rarely has the visibility of the prosecutor's, nor does it serve as a step on the political career ladder. Individual defense attorneys in private practice sometimes have significant political ties, but as a group, defense attorneys are poorly organized and without clout.

COURTS AND THEIR PUBLICS

Indirect ties to the communities that criminal courtrooms serve might be important to the court, but they are not extensive. There are no ties with victims of crime. Victims come to the courtroom and to the prosecutor's office as witnesses, but by their very circumstances, victims are unorganized and their links to the court are sporadic. Indeed, most victims dread their day in court and avoid anything more than the minimal contact their case requires. Likewise, the criminal courts have few links with the neighborhoods that produce most of the victims and offenders. The courts rarely are located in these areas; there is no outreach program to make the courts' work more easily understood by the people most involved. The courtroom workgroup does not even have strong ties within the criminal justice professional community. That community is fragmented into its component parts. Judges meet with other judges; prosecutors attend meetings with other prosecutors; defense counsel have their own associations. Rarely do all three join in a single group or systematically communicate with each other.

Occasionally, city leaders make formal requests to judges or prosecutors on the handling of particular kinds of cases. For instance, in

Minneapolis the mayor and city council sometimes have asked judges to deal more harshly with prostitutes, and apparently the courts responded affirmatively.[26] Police officials have also attempted to coordinate action plans in case riots erupt.[27]

The principal link that binds the criminal courtroom to the larger community is the media.[28] Newspapers and television reporters work the hallways and courtrooms of the courthouse for stories to spice up their daily reports. A symbiotic relationship often develops between courtroom workgroups and reporters. Workgroup members steer reporters to interesting cases, and reporters in turn often overlook (or allow themselves to be steered away from) events that might lead to criticism of the workgroup. Thus, the daily output of plea bargains and dismissals rarely attracts media attention, while the unusual trial of a grisly murder draws all the reporters. Nevertheless, this relationship between the workgroup and reporters usually fails to insulate the courtroom workgroup entirely. Occasional media criticism concerns workgroup members; they remember critical coverage for a long time and carefully save good notices of their performance in their clippings' files. This is particularly true of prosecutors, who feel the most vulnerable to public criticism because they are the most politically ambitious among the courtroom workgroup.

how courtrooms work

A number of quite different procedures take place in adjudicating criminal complaints. There may be *adversarial proceedings*. These are the trials most people are familiar with from their exposure to television dramas and newspaper accounts. But most charges are disposed of at hearings that have only some of the attributes of an adversarial proceeding. We call these *quasi-adversarial*. Finally, most convictions are the product of *dispositional proceedings*, which involve negotiations leading to guilty pleas. To understand who has influence in the dispensation of city justice, we have to examine each of these operational modes in detail.

ADVERSARIAL PROCEEDINGS

Adversarial proceedings have three principal characteristics: they are two-sided disputes, they follow rigid and formal rules, and a third party renders the decisions. In criminal prosecutions, the two sides are the state, represented by a state's attorney (also often called district attorney or prosecuting attorney) and the defendant, who is usually represented by another lawyer. No one else is represented directly in the case. The victim, for instance, is spoken for—if at all—by the prosecutor; the defendant's friends and family are represented—if at all—by the defense counsel.

The formal, rigid rules that govern adversarial proceedings are particularly distinctive. Everything must be done "by the book." This means that the charges must be written in proper form and follow the detailed rules specified by law. Evidence seized through illegal means may not be introduced. Evidence must be given in person and must be direct rather than secondhand. Each step of the proceedings must occur within the time period specified by law. All of the proceedings are recorded, and the record of the case may be inspected by an appeals court to determine its legality.

Judges or juries, not the parties themselves, make the final adjudicatory decisions in adversarial proceedings. Many trials are conducted by a judge alone, without a jury. The judge hears the evidence and decides not only the application of the law but also the guilt or innocence of the defendant. Such trials are called *bench trials*. In a small number of instances, defendants ask for a jury trial. Then ordinary citizens—usually twelve but sometimes as few as six—are called into the courtroom to hear the evidence and decide guilt or innocence. The jurors are supposed to follow the applicable law according to the instructions given them by the judge. In addition, during the course of a jury trial, the judge makes decisions about the admissibility of evidence, about the permissibility of questions attorneys ask witnesses, and about other legal matters.

Jurors are not representatives of the public in the same sense that legislators or elected executives are. The court chooses them at random, usually from a list of voters in the jurisdiction. All must serve unless they have a good excuse, such as persons who have small children at home or physicians whose work is considered indispensable. In addition, attorneys in the case question prospective jurors to determine whether they have prejudices that might make it difficult for them to hear the case fairly. For instance, someone who is married to a police officer or who has recently suffered from a similar crime to the one before the court would probably be excused. Jurors often serve at several trials over a period of a week or a month before they are replaced by a new random drawing from the voters' list. Although jurors are ordinary citizens with no formal ties to the courts, they are not representatives of the public because they have no formal links with other members of the community. Each set of six or twelve persons may reflect quite disparate views about crime and punishment. Further, no mechanisms exist to hold jurors responsible for their decisions. They can be punished only if they act dishonestly or permit themselves to be influenced by persons or events outside the courtroom.

Although adversarial proceedings have a formal, rigid structure, they are fraught with uncertainty, which results largely from dependence on persons outside the regular courtroom workgroup. For instance, the factual basis of decisions depends on the accounts provided by witnesses testifying on the witness stand. They respond to friendly questions from one attorney and unfriendly cross-examination from the other. Even with substantial preparation, witnesses tend to be unreliable. Some tell different stories on the witness stand than in the attorney's office; some get rattled or angry; some make a better impression than do others on such intangible matters as credibility or sincerity; some invite pity, and others evoke disgust. Compounding these uncertainties, prosecutors and defense counsel in most cases spend very little time interviewing witnesses to anticipate their performance. It is not at all uncommon to see both prosecutors and defense attorneys meet their witnesses for the first time minutes before the trial begins. Consequently, trials are full of nasty surprises.

Uncertainty also comes from the role of the jury. Jurors are largely unpredictable. Neither attorney knows any of them, and even substantial experience with jury trials tells the attorney only that he or she cannot fully predict or understand what the set of twelve persons will do.

This uncertainty is an inherent part of the adversarial process. It is also a principal reason why attorneys like to avoid adversarial proceedings if they can. Judges and juries do not totally control adversarial proceedings, however. Attorneys have some important resources they can use to influence the outcome of adversarial proceedings.

Prosecutors have the greatest amount of control. Their control resides in two resources: information and discretion. Prosecutors generally know more about the incident and charges than defense attorneys because they receive police reports and usually have a staff of investigators to fill any obvious gaps in the evidence. Evidence seized from the defendant (such as clothes with the appearance of blood or substances that look like narcotics) are analyzed by police laboratories. Any prior criminal record of the defendant is available from police computers. All or most of this information eventually must be revealed to the defense attorney, but the prosecutor has it first and most fully. Of course, the prosecution must prove beyond a reasonable doubt that the defendant committed the alleged crime, and therefore it has the greatest need for such information. Many defendants do not produce any evidence at all at a trial, confident that the state has not proved its case. Nevertheless, because the prosecution generally has more information than the defense, it has considerable influence over how a trial develops.

In addition, the prosecution has many discretionary powers. It can decide what charges to bring and, later, what charges to take to trial. For instance, a person may be charged with robbery, assault, and disorderly conduct. A prosecutor may decide to drop the assault and disorderly conduct charges and go to trial only on the robbery, or he or she may drop the more serious robbery and assault charges and go to trial on the disorderly conduct allegation. Prosecutors also control how much leniency they are willing to offer for a guilty plea. They may make an offer that a defendant cannot reasonably refuse and thereby preclude an adversarial trial. On the other hand, prosecutors may refuse to bargain, thereby ensuring a trial unless the defendant is willing to throw himself or herself on the mercy of the court.

But not all the cards are in the prosecutor's hand. Defense counsel also has substantial resources to affect trial. In most jurisdictions defendants have the option of choosing between a bench or jury trial. Jury trials generally take much longer and are more difficult, for both the prosecutor and the judge, so they are not indifferent to the choice a defendant makes. Moreover, the course of an adversarial proceeding is at the mercy of defense counsel. Counsel may object to the admissibility of evidence and force a hearing on the way it was seized. They may object to the way in which the prosecutor presents his or her evidence during the trial.

Note that victims have no formal role in the proceedings except as witnesses. Their influence is limited to appearing or disappearing. When they fail to appear, the case often must be dropped, and that happens frequently. Note also that the general public has no role except for occasional jury duty.

Full-blown adversarial proceedings are not the norm in criminal cases. On the contrary, in most cities they are the exception, making up only 10 percent of criminal cases. Most of these trials are not jury trials but bench trials, with the judge deciding both legal matters and the question of guilt.

A very large number of criminal charges is disposed of through attenuated adversarial proceedings; that is, hearings or court appearances that have some of the characteristics of a trial but not all. Formality is most frequently sacrificed. For instance, every day courts in large cities need to process hundreds of minor charges such as petty theft, disorderly conduct, or prostitution. They do so by cutting corners in a variety of ways. Defendants are sometimes advised of their rights in a group; twenty or thirty defendants are brought to the bench and their rights are read to them by the judge. The judge may then ask them collectively or individually whether they understand. In many misdemeanor courts, clerks schedule one case after another in rapid succession, allowing only seconds or minutes for each defendant. If the defendant is willing to plead guilty, the judge quickly accepts the plea and assesses the penalty, which in many instances is simply the time already served in jail awaiting the hearing. If the defendant is uncertain about what he or she should do and pleads not guilty, the case is scheduled for another day, when it receives the same rapid processing or is scheduled for the late afternoon when the judge and prosecutor can spend more time on it.[29]

Considerable informality also prevails at hearings that take place at various stages of processing criminal cases. When defendants face serious felony charges, they often have separate hearings for arraignment, at which the charges are read to them; for setting bond; for scheduling the preliminary examination, which determines whether there is "probable cause" for holding them to face a trial; and for hearings on the legality of the procedures used to seize the evidence against the defendants. These hearings often take place in crowded courtrooms amidst much confusion. Informal exchanges of information between attorneys and the judge are more characteristic of these hearings than the formal taking of evidence from duly sworn witnesses, although that also occurs sometimes.

These proceedings, however, retain some of the traits of adversarial hearings. The rigorous rules of the adversarial process are often invoked. They may be bent for the sake of speed, but prosecutors and defense counsel can resort to them at any time. The judge retains the decision-making role. In some hearings witnesses play a very important role, as, for example, when the admissibility of evidence is at stake. But jurors are not used in these quasi-adversarial proceedings.

In some cities such as Los Angeles, Baltimore, and Pittsburgh these proceedings are known as "slow pleas."[30] Guilty pleas resulting from explicit plea bargaining are rare. Instead, there is an abbreviated bench trial where the prosecutor and defense attorney hurry through the evidence or simply submit a transcript of earlier proceedings in place of fresh testimony. In Baltimore it is not uncommon to see the judge prod a prosecutor or defense attorney when the evidence is presented too slowly; after a half hour's proceedings, the judge renders a verdict. In most instances, the participants know what the result will be but prefer the ceremony of a bench trial with the decision of the judge to convict over a guilty plea by the defendant. In addition, the participants may not work closely enough with each other to facilitate explicit bargaining; therefore, they must resort to the bench trial slow plea to obtain convictions that could otherwise be procured through negotiations. Because the prosecutor and defense counsel know the judge's inclinations well in most instances, there is much less uncertainty in these slow pleas than in full-blown bench or jury trials.

DISPOSITIONAL PROCEEDINGS

Negotiations are the most common means of disposing criminal cases. Negotiations not only culminate in the widely known plea bargains, but they also characterize many of the preliminary and ancillary proceedings that occur as a case is processed.

Prosecutors and defense counsel are the typical participants in negotiations. Judges sometimes take a part; defendants on occasion are present during the negotiations and must give their explicit consent to the outcome of the negotiatons. Victims occasionally play a role, although that is more the exception than the rule.

Negotiations are sometimes quite formalized. In Detroit, for instance, every felony case is brought before a pretrial conference where a prosecutor who specializes in plea bargaining confers with the defense counsel in every case. Where the prosecutor's policy permits it, an offer is made to the defense attorney. If the attorney thinks it acceptable, he or she goes out in the hallway to confer with the client. If the client accepts the offer, he or she and the attorney immediately go to a courtroom where the plea is offered, accepted, and the defendant sentenced accordingly. If the plea is rejected, the case is scheduled for trial a few weeks later. Each case is allotted about twenty minutes in the pretrial conference. The prosecutor and defense attorney usually have not conferred on the case before, but they are likely to know one another from previous cases if the defense attorney is a regular criminal lawyer.[31]

In many cities negotiations are much less formalized. For instance, in Chicago prosecutors and defense counsel informally talk about a case whenever it is scheduled on the docket even though the trial is not imminent. The discussion is often tentative and desultory until both sides get a feel for what appears to be an acceptable compromise or until the case is ready for trial. Then, by implicit agreement, both parties signal the judge that they wish a conference, and the judge informs the defendant that he or she will hold a conference with the two attorneys unless the defendant objects. At the conference, which takes place in the judge's chambers, both sides state their case. Sometimes, the prosecutor indicates the sentence he or she would be willing to settle for; at other times, the judge indicates what the case is worth. The defense counsel rarely takes the initiative in indicating a price for an agreement. If the defense counsel finds the prosecutor's or judge's offer acceptable, he or she leaves chambers to talk to the client, often seeking to convince the client to accept the offer. If the offer is accepted, everyone files into the courtroom to accept the plea and sentence the defendant. If not, a trial is scheduled either for later in the day or for a day in the near future.[32]

More than informality and flexibility characterize negotiations. Their most important characteristic is that the prosecutor and defense counsel by and large control the proceedings. The judge plays a much smaller role than in trials. Ordinarily the judge has little discretion over whether to accept a guilty plea; often he or she is not even a party to the negotiations. Witnesses play no role whatsoever. The incident is reconstructed on the basis of reports and notes. The prosecutor often makes it out to be as grave as possible, while the defense attorney gives it the best possible interpretation and emphasizes extenuating circumstances. In this exchange, prosecutor and defense attorney completely control how information is revealed and how much is exposed. They often have worked together in previous cases and know each other well; the exchange is casual and informal but under the complete control of the participants. There are no surprises from recalcitrant or unreliable witnesses.

Plea bargaining varies considerably from city to city.[33] In some, as in Chicago, the bargaining focuses on the length of the sentence. Charges are rarely changed or dropped. In other cities like Cleveland, bargaining centers on the charges to which a defendant pleads guilty. The prosecutor may decide to drop some charges while accepting the plea on others. That requires no commitment from the judge about the length of the sentence, but it normally does limit possible sentences since some charges carry greater maximum sentences than others. Furthermore, sometimes the bargaining is entirely implicit. Defense attorneys (and occasionally defendants themselves) know what sentence the judge will mete out if a guilty plea is entered. They rely on that understanding alone without any explicit discussion between them and the prosecutor or judge.

Such implicit bargaining occurs more frequently in misdemeanor courts and in preliminary proceedings than just before felony trials.[34] These proceedings are more routine; they are more frequent; they provide more opportunity to rely on the judge's past performance. For instance, it is quite common for prosecutor and defense counsel to come to a quick agreement on a trial date or on a motion for discovery. The stakes may be high, but the understanding between the parties is so complete that no formal conferences are required to reach an agreement.

Plea bargaining does not take place in a vacuum; it is constantly influenced by the outcomes of trials. This occurs in several ways. For one thing, attorneys and their clients are unlikely to accept a prosecutor's offer if they believe on the basis of their recent experience or the experience of others that they will do better at trial. When the rules for trials change, the frequency of negotiation and its terms also change. For instance, in Baltimore in the late 1960s jury trials became more common as more blacks were called for jury duty. Black defendants—at least for a time—believed that they would do better before a jury of their peers than through negotiations with the prosecutor or by asking for a trial before a judge alone.[35] It is mistaken, however, to expect a direct link between the results of trials and the occurrence of negotiations. Communication in large-city courthouses is quite imperfect. Each week dozens of trials take place, but they occur in separate courtrooms and sometimes in buildings separated from each other by several miles. The results become known only through informal communication channels and largely by chance. Consequently, no one in the courthouse has good information about the current outcome of trials for particular offenses. Instead, courthouse regulars talk about the unusual and spectacular trials—the ones that also often capture the attention of the media. So, if a convicted murdered gets a 1,000 to 2,000 year sentence after a jury trial (as happened in 1977 in Chicago), that sticks in the minds of prosecutors, defense counsel, and defendants even though such a sentence is a freak and reflects the unusual circumstances of the case rather than a tendency toward extremely harsh sentences.[36]

Even a false assumption that judges penalize defendants who demand a jury trial or the belief that some judges (for example, visiting judges) are harsher than others may propel defendants to plead guilty or to accept the outcome of a slow-plea bench trial. One observer argues that such beliefs are the principal force leading to guilty pleas in cities like Pittsburgh and Minneapolis.[37] Others have sought to show that jury trials do not produce much harsher sentences than guilty pleas in cities like Baltimore, Chicago, and Detroit when one takes into account the more serious nature of the cases that go to jury trials.[38]

Guilty pleas or their slow-plea bench trial equivalents are the principal source of convictions in city trial courts. They are not a new phenomenon, however, and they are not the consequences of heavy caseloads. Historical research has revealed that guilty pleas were quite common in the late nineteenth and early twentieth centuries.[39] Today they are as common in cities where courts have a light caseload as in cities where the caseload is heavy.[40] While we do not know with certainty why dispositional proceedings have replaced adversarial trials, the most convincing set of causes seems to lie in the organizational context in which prosecutor, defense attorney, and judge work. If possible, they seek to reduce and control the uncertainty of their work. This can be accomplished much more effectively by plea bargaining than trials. Where working arrangements facilitate negotiations, they take place. Only where the participants cannot reduce uncertainty by negotiating—because they do not know each other well enough or because they have no opportunity to interact informally—do participants resort to quasi-adversarial proceedings or full-blown trials.

Consequently, while it is important to know what is going on in trials in order to understand negotiations, the two are not simply linked. When substantial changes occur in trials, negotiations are affected. Likewise, if one party to negotiations changes its outlook drastically, the pattern of cases going to trial is also likely to change.

what the criminal courts accomplish

The outcomes of these complicated proceedings vary considerably from city to city. Our information about outcomes is not very reliable, but some indications may be gleaned from the data summarized in table 5.1 In some cities, many (and sometimes most) cases are dismissed even after the considerable screening that the police do on the streets. That is, after some processing the defendant is unconditionally released. The proportion convicted also varies greatly, ranging from three-fourths in Los Angeles to one-fourth in Chicago. In every city, the proportion of all persons brought to criminal court who are eventually sent to prison is small; in none is it more than 30 percent and in most it ranges from 15 to 25 percent. In New York City, the proportion sent to prison is only 5 percent, although another 22 percent receive a jail sentence of less than a year.

Table 5.1, however, does not reflect all the punishment meted out to those who are initially brought to court. All of these persons suffer detention as a result of their arrest, and many of them spend

table 5.1
Crime Rates and Felony Dispositions
in Selected Cities

city	major crimes per 100,000 population[a]	percentage of felony defendants convicted	percentage of felony defendants sent to prison
Baltimore, Md.	5622	43.7[b]	27.6[b]
Chicago, Ill.	3614	25.6[b]	15.0[b]
Detroit, Mich.	7095	57.5[b]	20.0[b]
New Haven, Conn.	5193	48.9[c]	na
Hartford, Conn.	4175	49.3[c]	na
Winstead, Conn.	na	41.5[c]	na
Prairie City[g]	na	60.8[d]	30.2[d]
Los Angeles, Calif.	6257	79.8[e]	10.0[e]
New York, N.Y.	5501	55.7[f]	5.0[f]

[a] Federal Bureau of Investigation, *Uniform Crime Reports, 1972* (Washington, D.C.: Government Printing Office, 1973).

[b] James Eisenstein and Herbert Jacob, *Felony Justice* (Boston, Mass.: Little, Brown & Company, 1977), pp. 292–93.

[c] Milton Heumann, *Plea Bargaining* (Chicago, Ill.: University of Chicago Press, 1978), p. 34.

[d] David W. Neubauer, *Criminal Justice in Middle America* (Morristown, N.J.: General Learning Press, 1974), pp. 201–37.

[e] Peter W. Greenwood and others, *Prosecution of Adult Defendants in Los Angeles County: A Policy Perspective* (Santa Monica, Calif.: The Rand Corporation, 1973), pp. 38, 149.

[f] Vera Institute of Justice, *Felony Arrests: Their Prosecution and Disposition in New York City's Courts* (New York: Vera Institute of Justice, 1977), p. 1.

[g] Prairie City is a pseudonym for a city studied by several social scientists.

some time in jail before they are released pending disposition of their case. Some spend months in jail only to be released as the result of a dismissal or acquittal. Many of them must pay for lawyers or bond. Many lose time from work and some lose their jobs as the result of their arrest. Many have family difficulties that result from the court action. All suffer from some uncertainty about their fate while their cases slowly grind through the court system. In many instances their fate is not decided for many weeks and sometimes many months. Even in cities with high dismissal rates, none can know for sure that his or her case will be dismissed. Until it is, the possibility of going to prison hangs over the defendant and can cut him or her off from society at the next court date.[41]

Another important feature of the information in table 5.1 is that the pattern of dispositions in a city is not related to its crime rate. Some, such as Hartford, Connecticut, with a relatively low crime rate have a high conviction rate; but Los Angeles, with an even higher conviction rate, has a higher crime rate as well. Chicago has a relatively low crime rate and a low conviction rate. Los Angeles and New York have similar crime rates even though their conviction rates and imprisonment rates are very different.

Severity of sentences also varies dramatically from one city to another. Levin has shown that Minneapolis courts dealt much more harshly with convicted defendants than did courts in Pittsburgh.[42] Eisenstein and Jacob showed similar variation for Baltimore, Chicago, and Detroit. For instance, a convicted armed robber would typically receive a sentence of eighty-four months in Baltimore and forty-nine months in Chicago, but only thirty-five months in Detroit.[43]

The same crime does not draw the same sentence even in the same city. This should not surprise us since the statutes guiding judges usually permit considerable discretion. Moreover, the circumstances of the crime and the offender often vary considerably even when the act (for instance, an assault) is the same. These disparities, however, do not seem to be systematically linked to the defendant's race or income.[44] In some circumstances, blacks receive heavier sentences, but in others they receive lighter ones. The very wealthy may appear to receive lighter sentences (although Patty Hearst would dispute that), but there are very few convicted defendants who are anything but poor. Thus, there is too little variation in economic status among those sentenced by judges to test the effect of income on sentences.

Another important disparity in treatment is that accorded juveniles.[45] Young people—normally until they are sixteen or seventeen years old—go to special courts. They usually cannot be imprisoned beyond their seventeenth or eighteenth birthdays.

Juvenile courts handle a very substantial number of cases. In 1974 it was estimated that the nation's juvenile courts processed more than 660,000 cases through formal judicial hearings and disposed of another 584,000 informally. Fifty-five percent of the formal court hearings (which usually involved more serious matters) occurred in cities with more than one-quarter of a million population.[46]

When sentenced to a prison, juveniles are sent to special institutions that hold only other juveniles. As with adults, very few juveniles whom the court determines guilty of some offense go to prison. Most are released under some kind of supervision, either in a foster home or with a probation officer. The record of all proceedings against juveniles is typically held confidential. There is no press coverage of the proceedings, and the record a juvenile develops is for all practical purposes wiped out when he becomes an adult. Consequently, many first offenders in adult court are in fact veterans of the juvenile court system, but no one in the adult court knows that. If by chance they learn it, they are not permitted to give official recognition to it.

There is no evidence that harsher sentences are linked with more or less crime. One reason may be that in all cities criminals with long records receive the harshest prison terms while those who come to court with few or no prior convictions receive probation or short prison terms. As we saw in chapter 3, however, criminals commit more offenses early in their careers than later. Thus, the courts' policy of severely punishing veteran criminals may be counterproductive. It tends to imprison those who no longer commit many crimes and returns the most active criminals to the street.

conclusion

It would be wrong to conclude that the courts make no difference in solving the problem of crime. If there were no punishment, crime would probably increase sharply. It might also be true that draconian punishment would decrease crime rates. But variation in punishment in American cities seems to make little difference in the likelihood that crime will occur. As we have already seen, crime is the product of a complex social process. Punishment of convicted criminals by the courts is part of that process, but it is only a small part. It is clearly not the determining part.

Indeed, we need to recognize that criminal courts perform a

number of functions other than simply attempting to control the amount of crime. One such function is reassuring the public that criminals are punished and that criminal laws need to be taken seriously. That function does not require that all persons accused of crime be convicted and imprisoned. Rather, the public needs to be aware that some such persons are caught and punished. Consequently, it is useful that trials and exemplary sentences receive wide publicity and that dismissal rates and probationary sentences remain obscure.

Many of the dismissals, however, are likely to serve another function. They involve offenders and victims who know each other, live with each other, and must continue to have a relationship with each other. A temporary breakdown in their relationship is what brought them to court in the first place. What the court does for them is to restore order and balance to their relationship. Their situation might not be improved if the offender were punished; rather, they need to have the authorities help them restore an equilibrium. The arrest and temporary incarceration of the offender separates the parties until their tempers have cooled. Invocation of the criminal process may help the weaker party establish a new balance in the relationship, which can then totter along until a new crisis erupts some time in the future.

In addition, table 5.1 does not show the much larger number of people who go through misdemeanor courts. They are involved in minor offenses that do not entail great bodily harm or large sums of stolen money. Even more of these cases are dismissed or dealt with in summary pleas and light sentences. These cases serve largely to maintain order on the streets (keeping drunks and prostitutes in their place) and to keep social relationships on an even keel. This is recognized by those who work in such courts. Consider, for instance, the opinion of one Connecticut prosecutor in a lower court:

> Most of the stuff that comes through the court is garbage. You wonder if they should even be arrested in many instances, why the police even bother. . . . A husband gets into an argument with his wife, they call a cop . . . that kind of thing. Two neighbors get into a sort of back-fence type thing. . . . There have to be criminal laws to take care of this kind of thing, but so much of this is routine, small petty crime. Motor vehicle violations, you have a speeding case and another speeding case, and then you have a case where somebody got into a minor accident, and so he gets arrested, that is what I mean by all this minor garbage, and most of it is just minor stuff.[47]

Many individuals get into and out of trouble in these courts, but the general public knows almost nothing about their operation. They are part of the mechanism that keeps the seamy side of a city's life in check. Except when these courts break down in some spectacular way, however, little is heard from them.

notes

1 John Paul Ryan and others, *America's Trial Judges at Work: The Role of Organizational Influences* (New York: The Free Press, 1979), ch. 3.

2 This concept is more fully developed in James Eisenstein and Herbert Jacob, *Felony Justice* (Boston, Mass.: Little, Brown & Company, 1977), pp. 19–64.

3 Martin A. Levin, *Urban Politics and the Criminal Courts* (Chicago, Ill.: University of Chicago Press, 1977), pp. 46–59; Bradley C. Canon, "The Impact of Formal Selection Processes on the Characteristics of Judges—Reconsidered," *Law and Society Review*, 6 (1972), 579–89; John Paul Ryan, Allan Ashman, and Bruce D. Sales, "Judicial Selection and its Impact on Trial Judges' Background, Perceptions, and Performance" (paper prepared for the Western Political Science Association annual meeting, Los Angeles, March 1978).

4 Ryan, Ashman, and Sales, "Judicial Selection"; Kenneth N. Vines and Herbert Jacob, "State Courts and Public Policy" in *Politics in the American States*, 3d ed., ed. Jacob and Vines (Boston, Mass.: Little, Brown & Company, 1976), pp. 249–55.

5 Ryan, Ashman, and Sales, "Judicial Selection," p. 26.

6 Ibid, pp. 14, 22.

7 Levin, *Urban Politics*, pp. 48–59.

8 Wesley G. Skogan, "Party and Constituency in Political Recruitment: The Case of the Judiciary in Cook County, Illinois" (unpublished Ph.D. dissertation, Northwestern University, 1971).

9 Wallace S. Sayre and Herbert Kaufman, *Governing New York City* (New York: W. W. Norton, 1960), pp. 543–47.

10 Levin, *Urban Politics*, pp. 54–59.

11 Ibid., pp. 48–54.

12 Ryan, Ashman, and Sales, "Judicial Selection," pp. 28–33; Joel S. Ish, "Trial Judges: Their Recruitment, Backgrounds, and Role Perceptions" (paper delivered for the 1975 annual meeting of the American Political Science Association, San Francisco, September 1975), pp. 14–17.

13 Vines and Jacob, "State Courts," pp. 253–55.

14 In 1974, twenty-one prosecutors reported in a survey that they employed fifty or more assistants; another thirty-five indicated that they employed twenty-one to fifty deputies. See Patrick F. Healy, *National Prosecutor Survey* (Chicago, Ill.: National District Attorney's Association, 1977), p. 7.

15 This is less true for small towns. Cf. Herbert Jacob, "Judicial Insulation—Elections, Direct Participation, and Public Attention to the Courts in Wisconsin," *Wis-*

consin Law Review (1966), pp. 801–19. Note that in 1978, the three leading contenders for the Pennsylvania governorship were former prosecutors.

16 David W. Neubauer, *Criminal Justice in Middle America* (Morristown, N.J.: General Learning Press, 1974), p. 45.

17 James Eisenstein, *Counsel for the United States* (Baltimore, Md.: Johns Hopkins University Press, 1978).

18 Eisenstein and Jacob, *Felony Justice*, pp. 81–86; 114–17, 145–54; Lief Carter, *The Limits of Order* (Lexington, Mass.: Lexington Books, 1974), pp. 45–61.

19 Healy, *National Prosecutor Survey*, p. 11.

20 Eisenstein and Jacob, *Felony Justice*, pp. 87–91, 117–21, 155–60; Albert W. Alschuler, "The Defense Attorney's Role in Plea Bargaining," *Yale Law Journal*, 84 (1975), 1179–1311.

21 Edward O. Laumann and John P. Heinz, "Specialization and Prestige in the Legal Profession: The Structure of Deference," *American Bar Foundation Research Journal* (1977), pp. 155–216.

22 Neubauer, *Criminal Justice*, pp. 68–71; Joel Handler, *The Lawyer and His Community* (Madison: University of Wisconsin Press, 1967), pp. 39–42.

23 The total number is given in Michael R. Gottfredson, Michael J. Hindelang, and Nicolette Parisi, *Sourcebook of Criminal Justice Statistics, 1977* (Washington, D.C.: U.S. Department of Justice, Law Enforcement Assistance Administration, 1978), p. 36.

24 Anthony Platt and Randi Pollock, "Channeling Lawyers: The Careers of Public Defenders," in *The Potential for Reform of Criminal Justice*, ed. Herbert Jacob (Beverly Hills, Calif.: Sage Publications, 1974), pp. 239–50. Levin describes Pittsburgh as an exception; see *Urban Politics*, p. 76.

25 Jonathan Casper, *American Criminal Justice* (Englewood Cliffs, N.J.: Prentice-Hall, Inc., 1972), pp. 106–15; Jonathan Casper, *Criminal Courts: The Defendant's Perspective, Executive Summary* (Washington, D.C.: U.S. Department of Justice, Law Enforcement Assistance Administration, 1978), p. 8.

26 Levin, *Urban Politics*, pp. 106–7.

27 Isaac D. Balbus, *The Dialectics of Legal Repression* (New York: Russell Sage Foundation, 1973), pp. 119, 165–75, 193.

28 Eisenstein and Jacob, *Felony Justice*, pp. 92–95, 122–23, 166–67.

29 Maureen Mileski, "Courtroom Encounters: An Observation Study of a Lower Criminal Court," *Law and Society Review*, 5 (1971), 473ff; Milton Heumann, *Plea Bargaining* (Chicago, Ill.: University of Chicago Press, 1978), pp. 35–36; Malcolm Feeley, *The Process is the Punishment* (New York: Russell Sage Foundation, 1979).

30 Eisenstein and Jacob, *Felony Justice*, pp. 250–51; Levin, *Urban Politics*, pp. 80–81; Peter W. Greenwood and others, *Prosecution of Adult Defendants in Los Angeles County: A Policy Perspective* (Santa Monica, Calif.: The Rand Corporation, 1973), pp. 20–23; Lynn M. Mather, "The Outsider in the Courtroom: An Alternative Role for Defense," in *The Potential for Reform*, ed. Jacob, pp. 263–89.

31 Eisenstein and Jacob, *Felony Justice*, pp. 249–51.

32 Ibid., pp. 244–59; Heumann, *Plea Bargaining*.

33 Albert W. Alschuler, "The Prosecutor's Role in Plea Bargaining," *University of Chicago Law Review*, 36 (1968), 50–112.

34 Heumann, *Plea Bargaining*, pp. 35–46; Malcolm Feeley, *The Process is Punishment* (New York: Russell Sage Foundation, 1979).

35 Eisenstein and Jacob, *Felony Justice*, p. 296.

36 Ibid., p. 285.

37 Levin, *Urban Politics*, pp. 68–73, 82–83.

38 Eisenstein and Jacob, *Felony Justice*, pp. 237–39.

39 Heumann, *Plea Bargaining*, p. 28; Lawrence M. Friedman, "Plea Bargaining in the Light of Archival Data: A Study of Alameda County, California," (unpublished paper, 1978).

40 Heumann, *Plea Bargaining*, pp. 31–35; Malcolm Feeley, "The Effects of Heavy Caseloads," in *The Legal System* ed. Sheldon Goldman and Austin Sarat (San Francisco, Calif.: W. H. Freeman, 1978).

41 Eisenstein and Jacob, *Felony Justice*, pp. 271–74.

42 Levin, *Urban Politics*, pp. 92–93.

43 Eisenstein and Jacob, *Felony Justice*, p. 280.

44 Ibid., pp. 282–86; Levin, *Urban Politics*, pp. 93–95.

45 Lawrence E. Cohen, *Delinquency Dispositions: An Empirical Analysis of Processing Decisions in Three Juvenile Courts* (Washington, D.C.: U.S. Department of Justice, Law Enforcement Assistance Administration, 1975); Robert M. Emerson, *Judging Delinquents* (Chicago, Ill.: Aldine, 1969).

46 Jacqueline Corbett and Thomas S. Vereb, *Juvenile Court Statistics, 1974* (Washington, D.C.: U.S. Department of Justice, Law Enforcement Assistance Administration, n.d.), p. 10.

47 Milton Heumann, *Plea Bargaining* (Chicago, Ill.: University of Chicago Press, 1978), p. 38. Copyright 1978 by the University of Chicago Press.

criminal justice in new york, chicago, los angeles, and prairie city

*N*one of the elements of the criminal-justice process that we have described in the preceding chapters operates in isolation. General social processes work in somewhat similar ways in all cities. The concentration of common crimes among the poor and the young, the fear of crime by the elderly, police use of both aggressive and passive patrols, the high incidence of dismissals and guilty pleas in courts, the punishment of defendants who are not convicted, and the incarceration of only a select few are common to almost all American cities. These characteristics, however, interact with each other and with other elements of city life in intricate patterns that make each city appear distinctive. Each city has its own history of problems and attempted solutions that provide a veneer of individuality to the operation of its criminal-justice process. Each city has its own political process, which permits different groups to influence the operation of criminal-justice agencies. Cities also operate in different institutional contexts. Some are the center of large metropolitan areas in states that provide considerable support for urban services; others are located in states that do little for their cities. Some are independent cities, and others are suburbs. It is, therefore, valuable to examine a few cities in greater depth to learn how the various parts of the criminal-justice process work together and interact with other parts of the city's governmental and political life. In the following pages we shall examine in some detail the operation of the criminal-justice process in three of the nation's largest cities—New York, Chicago, and Los Angeles—and in a group of middle-sized cities that may represent another slice of urban life.

new york

New York prides itself on being the hub of the United States. Since New York is the nation's largest city and largest metropolitan area, its officials insist that it is also number one in commerce, finance, and culture. It also has the apparent distinction of being first in crime.

In 1976 New York police recorded 658,000 serious offenses; most of those were property crimes but a substantial number were crimes of violence.[1] This total amounted to 86 crimes for every 1,000 persons living in New York. As figure 6.1 indicates, this total represents an enormous increase over the preceding sixteen years; it was five times greater in 1976 than in 1960. That quintupling occurred during a period when the population did not grow. Some of the rise in crime statistics undoubtedly reflects changes in recording practices. For instance, between 1965 and 1966, crime statistics in New York almost doubled. That change was the result of the appointment of a new police commissioner and the adoption of new administrative procedures.[2] These events had little to do with the actual incidence of crime; the newly recorded crimes had probably always existed. The change in reporting practices, however, did not alter the steady growth of crime statistics in New York during the following ten years. Moreover, homicides—which are usually not underreported to any significant degree—almost quadrupled during the period 1960–76, until in 1976 an average of more than four killings occurred each day of the year.

The appearance of a very high crime rate in New York is reinforced by the city's position as the hub of the nation's news enterprises. The *New York Times* is the country's most prominent and influential newspaper; it is read throughout the nation, and its reports on New York crime make events in New York more prominent than they might be if they occurred elsewhere. Much the same occurs with the other media. Two of the three television networks originate their nightly news from New York; their reporters and anchors experience New York crime directly. The editorial offices of the nation's two largest weekly news magazines are also in New York.

fig. 6.1
Serious Offenses Known to the Police in New York City, 1960–76

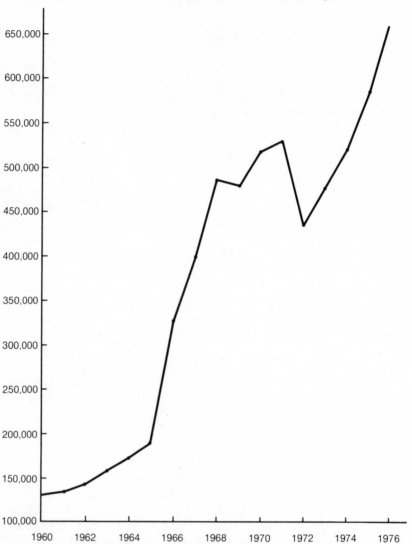

Source: Federal Bureau of Investigation, *Uniform Crime Reports, 1960–76* (Washington, D.C.: Government Printing Office, 1961–77).

Moreover, the volume of crime in New York is so great that every day incidents occur that may be portrayed in spectacular ways by the media. The whole nation witnessed the "Son of Sam" murders, the apprehension of David Berkowitz as their perpetrator, and his court appearances and sentencing. He was charged with committing a series of six apparently random murders. There was little to distinguish these murders, however, from the more than 1,600 other murders committed during the same period of time except that the media (abetted by the police) featured them. The slayings provided vivid reinforcement of the popular perception of New York as a dangerous place. In a similar fashion, when there was an electric power failure that blacked out much of New York in July 1977, widespread looting occurred. The apparent breakdown of law and order with the dimming of the lights again captured enormous attention from the nation's media. There is little indication that similar behavior would not occur in many other cities if they had a public utility as inept as New York's. Given the more than 40,000 thefts that ordinarily occur in New York during any single year, the looting during the blackout was scarcely unprecedented. But the blackout thefts came all at once in the glare of publicity, and so they reinforced the image of New York as a lawless city.

As in all large cities, the overall city statistics disguise important variations between neighborhoods. Crime rates in Harlem are much higher than in Staten Island. Prostitution is rampant around Times Square in Manhattan, but it cannot be found in most residential neighborhoods. However, even some wealthy neighborhoods have what appear to be high crime rates. For instance, the Upper East Side—an area extending from Central Park to the East River and serviced by a single police precinct—reported almost 10,000 felony crimes in 1977.[3]

The actual incidence of crime in New York, as in every city, is much higher than police statistics indicate. While in 1974 the police reported knowing about 68 crimes for every 1,000 residents, a survey of residents revealed approximately 111 crimes of comparable magnitude per 1,000 population.[4] Many of the crimes that the police did not record were not reported to them by victims. Others are incidents the police would not consider criminal.

As in every city the burden of crime did not fall evenly across New York's population.[5] The young were particularly heavily assaulted; 58 victimizations occurred for every 1,000 youngsters between the ages of 12 and 15. This compares to a rate of 40 per 1,000 for adults between the ages of thirty-five and forty-nine and a rate of

25 per 1,000 for senior citizens over sixty-five. On the other hand, middle-aged persons had a much higher rate of theft victimization than either the young or old. In terms of income, the poor had the highest victimization rate for crimes of violence, and the rich were most often the prey of property crimes.[6] In New York the distribution of crime was widespread enough that every stratum of the population suffered. No socioeconomic group reported such a low victimization rate that it could be untroubled by the crime problem.

Nevertheless, crime was perceived as a more serious problem by New York's poor than by its affluent residents. Although a remarkable 45 percent of those surveyed with less than $3,000 annual income felt that their neighborhood was less dangerous than others in the metropolitan area, 76 percent of those with more than $25,000 annual income gave the same answer. At the same time, 40 percent of those with low incomes felt reasonably safe when out in their neighborhood alone at night; 61 percent of the wealthy felt the same way.[7] In both instances it is important to note that while there were very large differences in perception between the poor and the wealthy, a sizable segment of the wealthy felt threatened by crime: 24 percent (or 56,000 persons) felt they did not live in the safest neighborhood and 37 percent (or 98,000 persons) did not feel safe at night.[8] Thus, it is not surprising that during much of this period crime was considered one of the most important issues in municipal politics, as evidenced both in public opinion surveys and by issues raised in city election campaigns.

One reason for the prominence of crime in city politics has been the position of the New York City police. It is a formidable force, consisting of almost 37,000 employees in 1976, 16,000 of whom were patrol officers.[9] The largest portion of that force consists of uniformed officers who belong to a local union, the Patrolman's Benevolent Association. Being a police officer is a well-paid occupation; New York police salaries began at $13,673 and rose to a maximum of $17,458 for patrol officers in 1978.[10] These salary figures do not include substantial fringe benefits in the form of health insurance and pensions. Although New York police do not earn as much as those in some other cities, their position is a desired one. In New York, as in many other cities, it is a job held by a disproportionate number of Irish-Americans. Blacks and other new minorities have had more limited access to police jobs. When blacks became a significant force in New York politics, civil-service reforms had made entry into the police force more difficult. It now requires a high-school diploma, good physical condition, and no police record. Given the good pay and security of police work, positions on the New York force are still much sought after, especially by members of ethnic groups whose other opportunities are relatively limited. The large size of the police force, its drain on the city budget, the prominence of the police union, and the competition for police jobs all contribute to keeping New York's police in the limelight.

The New York police consider themselves an independent force even though the police commissioner is appointed by the mayor and each new mayor usually appoints a commissioner. But the force is made up of career officers who resent political interference. That is particularly true when such interference appears to subject police officers to the scrutiny of civilians who do not share their outlook on law and order. This became most clearly evident in the 1960s when Mayor Lindsay appointed a civilian review board to look into complaints about abuses of police power. The Policeman's Benevolent Association staged a vigorous electoral campaign against the board and won a referendum repealing it. That victory returned the investigation of complaints to the police department itself and excluded civilian outsiders from judging police officers' work.

That action, however, did not remove the police from the political limelight, in part because reports of corruption within the police force have recurred. Corruption, as we have seen, is an endemic problem for the police. It also highlights the difficulties involved in imposing effective control over police officers in their daily work.

The problem is well illustrated by the investigation of police corruption in New York undertaken by the Knapp Commission on the heels of revelations by plainclothes officer Frank Serpico of systematic extortion and bribery in the enforcement of gambling laws.[11] Serpico found upon his assignment to a plainclothes detail that his colleagues were operating a "pad" that produced monthly payments of $800 for each man on the detail. Serpico refused to participate; his efforts to get higher police officials to investigate and to stop these practices were fruitless until he went to the *New York Times* with his story. Even then the investigation remained shallow and did not seek to discover the connections between corruption at the patrol level and involvement by lieutenants, captains, and higher police officials. The Knapp Commission's conclusions were devastating:

> We found corruption to be widespread. It took various forms depending on the activity involved, appearing at its most sophisticated among plainclothesmen assigned to enforcing gambling laws. . . . Corruption in narcotics enforcement lacked the organiza-

tion of the gambling pads, but individual payments—known as "scores"—were commonly received and could be staggering in amount. . . . Corruption among detectives assigned to general investigative duties also took the form of shakedowns of individual targets of opportunity. . . . Uniformed patrolmen assigned to street duties were not found to receive money on nearly so grand or organized a scale, but the large number of small payments they received present an equally serious if less dramatic problem. . . . Sergeants and lieutenants who were so inclined participated in the same kind of corruption as the men they supervised. In addition, some sergeants had their own pads from which patrolmen were excluded. . . . Although the Commission was unable to develop hard evidence establishing that officers above the rank of lieutenant received pay-offs, considerable circumstantial evidence and some testimony so indicated.[12]

The report continues, detailing the resistant attitude of the police department in acknowledging corruption as a severe problem:

The interaction of stubbornness, hostility, and pride has given rise to the so-called "rotten-apple" theory. According to this theory, which bordered on official Department doctrine, any policeman found to be corrupt must promptly be denounced as a rotten apple in an otherwise clean barrel. It must never be admitted that his individual corruption may be symptomatic of underlying disease.[13]

As the commission indicated, it appears unlikely that the command structure of the police department was totally unaware of what was going on. Yet higher police officials were not charged with participation. At the very top the impact of the investigation was finally felt when the police commissioner resigned and the new commissioner, Patrick Murphy, brought into police headquarters an almost entirely new staff.

Since the Knapp Commission report, individual instances of corruption continue to be reported in the press, especially those involving courts and judges as well as police. Few of these have resulted in successful criminal prosecutions, but they have kept the police in the public eye.

The Knapp Commission's revelations of deep-seated corruption did not result in widespread loss of confidence in the New York police by city residents. Not long after the commission's report, New Yorkers were asked, "Would you say in general that your local police are doing a good job, an average job, or a poor job?" Seventy-four percent indicated that the police were doing a good or average job; only 15 percent said the police were doing a poor job.[14] While that 15 percent is somewhat higher than in other cities (in eight other cities the number is 10 percent), it indicates that most New Yorkers retained confidence in their police despite the unfavorable publicity that had engulfed them in the preceding months.

With 16,000 officers and a yearly sum of more than 600,000 serious crimes known to the police, a staggering number of cases are brought to New York's criminal courts. The prosecutorial staff and the courts that handle this tidal wave are organized in a much more complex pattern than the police. While the police operate under a unified command throughout the city and are ultimately responsible to the mayor, who is elected citywide, the courts and prosecutorial staffs are divided into separate borough (county) jurisdictions. In each of the city's five boroughs, a district attorney is elected; each borough also has its own set of courts for handling criminal cases.

As long as a strong party organization existed that could hold the separate borough factions together, political influence could coordinate the policies of the five district attorneys. But New York has lacked such a strong party organization for decades, with the result that each district attorney is a political power in his or her own right. For many years the most prominent post—the one in Manhattan—was held by Frank Hogan who held himself to be independent. He outlasted mayors and other officials and ran his office in his own way. To a lesser degree, the other district attorneys exercised similar independence.

There is no public defender in New York. Rather the Legal Aid Society contracts with the courts to represent indigent defendants. Like the district attorney's offices, this is a very large operation with hundreds of attorneys. It operates in all the boroughs.

Two sets of judges hear criminal cases. Judges of the criminal court hear minor cases and preliminary proceedings in felony cases; in 1978 there were seventy-seven such judges.[15] They are appointed for a set term by the mayor and have long been used as patronage appointments in return for loyal service in support of the mayor's party faction. Judges hearing felony cases are elected to the supreme court, a title used in New York to designate trial courts, not the highest appellate court as in most other states. In 1978, 120 supreme court justices were assigned to criminal proceedings.[16] Supreme court judges run on a partisan ballot. In New York City this means that they generally must win endorsement from the party's nominating caucus.

Party factions often hotly contest judicial positions because they are seen as important patronage plums. That does not mean that the persons who win office have little merit. But in addition to merit as a potential judge, lawyers seeking the bench in New York must have good political connections and must usually have contributed financially or otherwise to political campaigns. In recent years more use has been made of citizen or lawyer screening panels to examine judicial candidates before their appointment or slating. There is no evidence, however, that such panels have substantially changed the character of those who go on the bench.

As in most cities, New York courts dispose of a large number of cases by dismissing them. Another very substantial number are completed with convictions but no prison sentences. In 1971, for instance, only one-quarter of all felony arrests resulted in jail time for the defendant, and only in one-fifth of those cases did the defendant receive felony time—that is, a sentence to a state prison rather than to the city jail.[17] Forty-four percent of all cases resulted in outright dismissal or acquittal. Since many crimes are not reported to the police and many of those reported do not result in an arrest, these statistics make clear that in New York, as in much of the rest of the country, most crimes do not result in substantial punishment.

Those punished, however, have tended to receive more severe sentences than in the past.[18] In part this is due to the initiation in New York, as in some other cities, of a special unit in the district attorney's offices for prosecuting repeat offenders. Defendants identified as career criminals are prosecuted with special vigor and are more likely to be convicted and to receive substantial sentences. That, of course, reinforces the tendency to incarcerate offenders who are past the peak of their career; youthful, first offenders are much less likely to receive harsh punishments even though they may be in the midst of committing more crimes than their "career" counterparts. The longer sentences are also in part apparently due to judicial awareness of public criticism of the alleged "softness" of the courts. Consequently, 52 percent of all felony convictions in New York City in 1977 resulted in prison sentences, about twice the proportion for the rest of the state; this is an increase of 9 percent from 1971.[19] Sentences themselves are said to have doubled in length. Waiting time from arrest to trial dropped from two years to an average of nine months. The number of persons convicted also rose, from 7,021 in 1970 to 12,208 in 1977.[20]

There is no evidence that the increasing harshness of New York City courts had any effect on the city's crime rate. It is perhaps symbolic of the lack of relationship between criminal activity and court action that the same issue of the *New York Times* that reported the harsher sentences made a front-page feature of the rising crime rate in the swank Upper East Side neighborhood. With crime as commonplace as it is in New York, small effects tend to become obscured. It requires a massive shift for an effect to be noticeable, and such a change has not yet occurred.

One other element of the criminal-justice process in New York must be considered. New York operates a large jail system that has been overcrowded and severely criticized by citizen commissions and by the federal courts for abominable conditions. As a consequence, there is considerable pressure to limit the number of persons held in jail before trial, to speed the trial process, and to restrict the number of persons incarcerated after trial in city jails. Part of the larger proportion of convicted defendants sent to state prisons may be attributable to that pressure. Even more evident, however, is the proliferation of diversion programs, which attempt to keep persons accused or convicted of relatively minor offenses out of jail and in the community under some kind of supervision.

Within the framework of everything that goes on in New York, providing criminal justice becomes top priority only when it poses a crisis to the rest of the city's operations. In the midst of a scandal in the police department, the mayor and his chief assistants and the media pour attention on it. In the aftermath of a spectacular crime or in the midst of a riot, all eyes turn to it. But most of the time other problems demand attention, and the criminal-justice process is allowed to proceed at its own pace and in its own way. Indeed, some other problems even force their own constraints on the criminal-justice process. For instance, the city's fiscal crisis in the mid-1970s prevented any expansion of the police force or major capital improvements in the correctional facilities. Periodic mayoral campaigns keep crime fighting in the public eye, however, as candidates vie in their efforts to impress voters with their promises to initiate more effective programs.

Within such contraints the work of criminals, the police, and the courts appear to continue on their own individual tracks. The activity of criminals does not appear to be affected substantially by what the police or courts do. When there is a drive to limit crime on the subways, robbers who operated on them appear to move to the buses or neighborhoods. When the police crack down on prostitution in one area, it seems to move to another. The potential pool of offenders appears to be so large in a city like New York that nothing contemplated by current public policy substantially reduces the crime rate. The crime rate, of course, might be much higher without existing police and court policies, but we have no way of knowing that with certainty.

At the same time, the police and courts each go their own way with little coordination between the two. New York's police—like their counterparts in other cities—are not evaluated on the basis of what happens to people they arrest. Their concern is with arrests themselves; apparently they must meet certain quotas.[21] As long as patrol officers make their arrests, their superiors will not bother them. They know that many of their arrests will not be pursued in court. That may anger them, but it does not alter their behavior. The courts, for their part, proceed with little concern about the effect of their decisions on policing. Prosecutors, judges, and defense attorneys are concerned with the outcome of individual cases and the dispensation of justice to individual defendants. The systemic, overall effect is consequently not the result of some overall policy but simply the accumulation of many particular decisions. New York, like all American cities, lacks a commissioner of justice who oversees the operation of the entire criminal justice process. The city has no mechanism for developing or executing an overall policy.

chicago

In Chicago crime policy is more readily coordinated. That is not the result of a more streamlined governmental structure. Rather, it is the consequence of domination by a political machine.

Chicago is known as the Second City. It is second in size to New York, although it has not always been second in crime, at least in popular perceptions. During the heyday of Prohibition, the capers of Al Capone and the gang wars that erupted in such bloody incidents as the St. Valentine's Day Massacre gave Chicago the reputation of being the capital of crime in the United States. In more recent years Chicago has promoted itself as "the city that works" in contrast to New York, which became known as "the Fun City" but was continually troubled by fiscal and political difficulties. Most of all, Chicago was known as the last major American city dominated by a political machine. All of these characteristics are borne out to some degree when we look at Chicago crime and the way the city has fought it.

The total crime rate as viewed from police statistics was considerably lower in Chicago in 1976 than in New York; 68 crimes were known to the police per 1,000 population, in contrast to New York's 86. Chicago's crime rate rose somewhat more rapidly than New York's in the period from 1960 to 1976. For the most serious crimes—murders—New York's rate rose much more rapidly, however. In 1960 Chicago with only one-third of New York's population had 25 more homicides; by 1976, Chicago had only two-thirds of New York's homicides. The homicide rate in Chicago was still higher than in New York, but New York had come a long way in closing the gap.[22]

With an average of more than three murders a day and dozens of robberies and other major crimes, Chicagoans get the impression that their city is dangerous. Many still remember Richard Speck's cold-blooded murder of seven nurses in 1966. Nothing equally chilling occurred in the following decade, but brutal killings and wanton assaults occupy some space in every day's newspapers and television newscasts.

No segment of Chicago was entirely free from violent crimes and household burglaries, but much of it was concentrated in a few areas. Chicago is a vast city with dozens of distinct neighborhood communities. The highest crime rates occurred in the south side and west side communities, which are densely packed with low income residents—blacks, Latinos, and Appalachian whites. But there were hundreds of blocks of middle-class housing for these same ethnic groups with low crime rates. Crime rates were also low in the Swedish, Irish, Croatian, German, Italian, Polish, Jewish, Korean, and many other middle-class ethnic neighborhoods that dot Chicago. While crime was a daily accompaniment of life in Chicago's ghetto communities, it rarely occurred in its middle-class neighborhoods.

Estimated crime rates for particular ethnic and age groups tell these differences dramatically. In 1975, young white males between the ages of fourteen and twenty-five had an estimated assault victimization rate of 707 per 100,000 and a robbery victimization rate of 636 per 100,000. The rate for young blacks was 1,870 for assaults and 1,827 for robberies; for Latinos it was 1,083 for assaults and 867 for robberies.[23] That meant that white youths were only one-half to one-third as prone to assaults and robberies as their counterparts in the black and Latino communities. Moreover, in every ethnic group, the victimization rate for youths was much higher than for the rest of the population.

Not only victims but also offenders are concentrated among

young ethnic-minority males. The frequency of offenders among black and Latino youth was much greater than among white youth, and the rate for youths was much higher than for the rest of the population.[24]

The character of violent crime in Chicago changed in important ways between 1965 and 1976. In the earlier period, three-quarters of the murders occurred among people who knew each other; they were the result of barroom and bedroom brawls. By 1975 that had changed substantially. Only 58 percent of the homicide victims were acquainted with their assailant.[25] Two important developments occurred during the decade to bring about this change. First, gun use increased dramatically. When guns are used rather than simply displayed, the likelihood of death is much higher than with other weapons. The second development involved the outcome of armed robberies. By 1975, armed robberies accounted for 22 percent of all homicides in Chicago instead of the 8 percent of ten years earlier.[26] Thus, violent crime spread from circles of acquaintances to strangers. These statistics reflect a situation that many people intuitively felt: crime had become more random, and life in the city consequently appeared to be more dangerous.

This perception of crime was reflected in attitudes of Chicagoans about crime in the mid-1970s. Across every income group and among whites as well as blacks, at least one-third of those surveyed indicated that they felt that crime had increased in their neighborhood over the past year or two.[27] Among Chicago whites, the same proportion of the very poor and the very rich felt that crime had increased in their neighborhood. Among Chicago blacks, more wealthy than poor persons felt that crime had increased. Fear of crime also had a broad impact on the lives of Chicagoans. A substantial proportion of all but young males reported that their activities were limited because of the fear of crime.[28] The fact that young males felt least inhibited is ironic because they were the most frequent victims of crime in Chicago. Perhaps they were the most victimized group because they were relatively fearless and willing to take high risks.

Thus, as in New York, crime was a very visible and worrisome problem for Chicagoans. When the crime rate appeared to turn downward during 1978, that announcement made page one of the *Chicago Tribune*. Likewise, apparent crime waves—such as were thought to occur on the rapid-transit system earlier in 1978—commanded the attention of the media and the public.

Chicago's resources for combating crime are quite different from

New York's. The "city that works" has not suffered from the same fiscal crisis as New York. It has enjoyed much stronger political leadership. Its criminal justice agencies are much less fragmented.

Chicago avoided the fiscal crisis that plagued New York most prominently but also affected such cities as Cleveland. One reason is that welfare expenditures are a state responsibility in Illinois rather than a city burden. Consequently, the rise in welfare expenditures that bore heavily on New York did not substantially affect Chicago. In addition, personnel expenditures were held in closer check in Chicago than in New York, where city workers organized into unions and won collective-bargaining rights. For instance, while Chicago's police had higher minimum and maximum salaries in 1978 than New York's, they needed eleven steps to reach the maximum in Chicago. There were only three steps from minimum to maximum in New York. The result was that in 1975 New York spent $9.24 per person on police protection and Chicago spent $7.67.[29] Chicago spent almost $5 million less for police protection than it would have at New York's expenditure rate. Similar savings held true for some other city services. The consequence was that Chicago had more financial slack to deal with problems and to adopt innovations. Chicago avoided the crisis atmosphere that pervaded New York government during most of the 1970s. It was never on the brink of bankruptcy; it never had difficulty meeting its payroll.

The second major difference from New York was the strong leadership that Mayor Daley provided Chicago for more than twenty years. Chicago was the last of the big cities governed by a political machine. The Daley machine dominated electoral campaigns at the city and county levels and exerted considerable influence over state and presidential elections as well. The key to Mayor Daley's power was that he combined party leadership with control over city policy making and administration. He and his allies held a tight reign over ward organizations, which in turn controlled the election of the city council. The city council became a rubber stamp for the mayor's will. Most legislation originated with the mayor, and almost no bill passed without his tacit approval. At the same time the mayor was chairman of the Cook County Democratic Party and through that mechanism was able to extend his control to county offices, which were won by Democrats. Democrats were not always successful in winning countywide offices; the suburbs of Chicago have a substantial Republican vote. By pushing its city wards for high voter turnouts, however, the machine managed to win control over most county offices during Daley's tenure.

Occasionally Republicans won the sheriff's office or the office of state's attorney, but their potential for danger was often neutralized by strong Democratic control over the County Board, which controlled the budgets of these offices.

Not only was Daley's leadership strong, but it was also continuous. Instead of a succession of mayors—each bringing a new set of close advisers and high officeholders to city hall—Chicago had Daley, Daley, and more Daley from 1955 until his death in 1976. This continuity was reflected in a high degree of stability in the most important administrative positions in Chicago's government, including the police department. Only one major change of police leadership occurred during Daley's administration.

That change, however, reflected the similarity of some of Chicago's problems to New York's. When Daley reached out to the University of California for Orlando Wilson to become police superintendent, he did so because his police department had sunk into one of the biggest scandals of Chicago's history. It had been revealed that some of Chicago's police officers moonlighted as burglars; it was no coincidence that they had good protection and their jobs were rarely interrupted by other officers. Other corruption was also rife within the department. For instance, Chicago drivers were used to folding a $5 or $10 bill around their driver's license when stopped for a traffic violation; such thoughtfulness brought them a reprimand instead of a ticket. Daley brought Wilson to Chicago to reorganize the department thoroughly. That is what Wilson did. When Wilson retired, one of his protégés took over. The Wilson administration of the police department cleaned the ranks and comprehensively reorganized and modernized the police force. Few Chicagoans pretend that corruption has ceased to be a problem. One still hears reports of traffic tickets being fixed on the street, and police up to the rank of precinct captain have been charged and convicted of accepting bribes. As in New York, police corruption is a continuing problem. But with the exception of the scandals that brought Wilson to Chicago, corruption has not altered the structure of the criminal-justice system.

Unlike New York, the criminal-justice system operates in a relatively coordinated fashion in Chicago. That is not the result of governmental centralization; the police are run by the city, and the prosecutor's office and the courts are run by the county. Rather, coordination has resulted from the dominance of the Daley machine. A Daley-dominated county board controlled the budget of the prosecutor's office and the courts. In addition, Daley controlled the election of the state's attorney and judges much of the time.

The close connection between city politics and the criminal-justice system in Chicago during the Daley era can be illustrated in many ways. For several years one of Daley's main rivals, Benjamin Adamowski, was state's attorney, elected on the Republican ticket after bolting Daley's Democratic machine. Adamowski embarrassed Daley with disclosures of scandals in traffic court and in the administration of bail. He was also the state's attorney who pressed the police scandal that forced Daley to recruit Orlando Wilson to reform Chicago's police. A few years later when the state's attorney post was again safely in Democratic hands, the new state's attorney found some potentially embarrassing ambiguities in Adamowski's use of office contingency funds and the media learned of them just as Adamowski began to campaign as a candidate against Daley. These disclosures had a damaging effect on his efforts to unseat Daley. In 1969, another state's attorney, Edward Hanrahan (who had been elected by the machine), caused great difficulty for Daley by raiding an apartment in which Black Panther leader Fred Hampton and others were sleeping. They allegedly shot their way into the apartment, killing Hampton and another leading Panther figure and wounding several others. At first the raiding party claimed they acted in self-defense, but upon later investigation it appeared that only one shot was fired from inside the apartment; all the others came from the raiders. Chicago's black community was furious, and the machine eventually withheld its endorsement from Hanrahan when he sought reelection. His replacement—an obscure traffic judge—did not win the primary, but Hanrahan lost the general election. That meant that the Daley machine once more lost control of the state's attorney's office to a Republican and that Daley had won the enmity of another rival. However, it is telling of Daley's influence even in the waning years of his administration that all the convictions of corruption tainting his administration came at the hands of the United States attorney's office—appointed by the Republican national administration of Richard Nixon —rather than at the hands of the local Republican district attorney. James Thompson, the United States attorney, won convictions against former governor Otto Kerner (who was then sitting as a United States court of appeals judge), against the county clerk, and against the floor leader of the city council—all close allies of the mayor. Thompson used these court victories against Mayor Daley's machine to propel himself into the governor's office in Illinois. But those blows to the Daley machine did not disturb it fundamentally; it continued to flourish untouched by the local state's attorney.

The courts were also dominated by Daley personnel. Only a few judges were close protégés of the mayor, but most judges elected from the city had to have political credentials that generally involved prior service to the Democratic party. Many judges worked their way up from assistant prosecutor (when the head post was held by a Democrat) or from positions in city agencies; others were lawyers who contributed their time and service to the party. The key judicial positions, however, were held by distinct loyalists. For instance, the chief judge of the criminal division was for a long time a former law partner of the mayor's; the chief judge of the entire court was also a long-time ally of the mayor. Control over such administrative positions in the judiciary was important to the machine because it assured the mayor that politically unreliable judges would not hear sensitive cases.[30] Republican judges elected from the outlying suburbs or blue-ribbon candidates whose loyalty was uncertain were assigned to hear personal injury or divorce cases rather than matters that might challenge city policy. Having loyalists in administrative positions in the Cook County Circuit Court also allowed the mayor to avoid embarrassment from judges who attracted unfavorable publicity. Judges who were visibly too lenient in criminal cases could easily be transferred to another division of the circuit court. Once there was a criminal court judge who employed his wife as a pistol-packing bailiff; he was quickly transferred to a less visible position when that practice attracted the attention of the Chicago media.

Chicago-style politics affected the courts in still another way; it helped mold the way plea negotiations proceeded.[31] As in many cities, the criminal courts disposed of most cases through guilty pleas that were the result of a negotiation process. In Chicago these negotiations proceeded in a very informal, unstructured way with the judges playing an important role. In felony cases negotiations took place intermittently from the time a defendant was arraigned until the day set aside for the trial. Cases were usually set down on the docket at monthly intervals and were routinely continued three or four times. Each of the case's appearances on the docket provided an opportunity for the assistant state's attorney and the defense counsel to talk about the case and its eventual disposition. Each side tried the other out, making dispositional suggestions reflecting the strength of the case and other circumstances surrounding it. After several such casual conversations, both sides found themselves ready for a serious conversation and asked for a conference with the judge. With the formal consent of the defendant, the attorneys then went into the judge's chamber, where the negotiation proceeded. Typically, the state's attorney first related what the charges were, how the incident arose, what aggravating circumstances existed (such as prior criminal record), and what he recommended as a sentence upon a guilty plea. The defense attorney then responded with the client's version of the incident and with an account of mitigating circumstances and his or her view of what an acceptable sentence might be. Often these two accounts proceeded in a quiet conversation, with one attorney frequently interrupting the other. The judge often interjected questions and comments. Finally many judges indicated what they considered to be an appropriate sentence. The defense attorney then left the chambers to confer with the client, who had been waiting in the courtroom all this time. If the defendant accepted the sentence, everyone came back into the courtroom to accept the guilty plea and formally pass the sentence. If the defendant refused the sentence or wanted to think about it, the case was postponed for several days or weeks; further negotiations might be needed until the case was disposed of or a trial actually held. Partisan politics played no role in these negotiations; precinct-committee members had no apparent influence in the process. The style of negotiation was very much like what occurred in other phases of Chicago's political arena, however, and it was no accident that the key participants in these proceedings—judges and assistant state's attorneys—were participants in that larger political arena. Unlike the process in some other cities—for instance, Detroit or Los Angeles—negotiations were informal rather than formal. This is an example of how the city's political culture permeates the criminal-disposition process.

The role of blacks and other minorities in the criminal-justice system, moreover, remained weak, as it was in the general political arena. Few blacks and almost no Latinos penetrated the upper ranks of the criminal-justice system either in the police department, the state attorney's office, the public defender's office, or the judiciary. Blacks and Latinos were overrepresented only as defendants and victims. There is no evidence that minorities were dealt with more harshly than whites, but some policies clearly affected them more severely. For instance, in July 1978, the chief judge announced that bail money put up for indigents would henceforth be used to help defray the expense of any public-defender services the defendant used. The policy meant that families putting up bond for their relatives lost their deposit. Such a policy clearly discouraged the posting of bail for indigent defendants and taxed them heavily. As most blacks and other minorities were poor, such a policy affected them most severely. Yet when the policy was announced, no public protest appeared in the media; Chicago's black community appeared powerless to prevent its implementation.

Thus, in many ways the criminal-justice system in Chicago reflected the characteristics of the city's political life. It was dominated by the Daley machine; its decision-making mode reflected the practices of the broader political arena; those powerless within the city in general were also weak in the criminal-justice process. Like Chicago government, the criminal-justice system was integrated by the political machine.

los angeles

Crime and the city's response to it also reflected political realities in Los Angeles, but those realities were quite different from Chicago's. Los Angeles is to many the symbol of nonpartisan, professional, managerial government. The city also possesses a highly fragmented political structure that lacks the cohesive bonds of a dominant political machine. At the same time, it harbors large concentrations of destitute inhabitants who commit and are victims of many crimes.

The total crime rate in Los Angeles was nearer New York's than Chicago's in 1976; 80 crimes per 1,000 inhabitants were known to Los Angeles police.[32] However, that rate was composed more of property crimes than was the case in the other cities. Indeed, the murder rate was only two-thirds that of Chicago. Crime grew faster in Los Angeles than in the other two cities. In 1960, the crime rate according to police statistics was 11 per 1,000 inhabitants; by 1976 it had risen to 80 per 1,000. The public's information about the rise of crime indicated to Los Angeles residents that crime was a rapidly growing threat to the pleasant life they were accustomed to.

The results of victimization surveys illustrate the predominance of property crime in Los Angeles, which criminologists have associated with sunbelt cities. For crimes of theft, burglary, and household larceny, Los Angeles had substantially higher victimization rates in 1974 than Chicago or New York.[33] In most other respects, Los Angeles was not different in the distribution of crime and victims among its population. The young were most victimized; the elderly, the least. Members of minority groups predominated among both offenders and victims.

As in the other cities, most residents in the early 1970s felt that crime was an increasingly serious problem. In Los Angeles, three-fifths felt that their chances of being attacked or robbed had gone up.[34] Forty-one percent of the white respondents and 51 percent of the black respondents felt that their neighborhood was unsafe at night.[35] But many more Los Angeles residents expressed confidence in their police. Fifty-four percent felt their police did a good job, as compared to 34 percent in New York and 45 percent in Chicago, where Mayor Daley insisted that the police were the finest in the country.[36] That difference reflects a substantial distinction in substance and style of city politics of the three cities.

As a relatively new city, Los Angeles has a less deeply rooted tradition of patronage politics; city jobs were used to a much lesser degree as the means of entering the mainstream of American life in Los Angeles than in New York and Chicago. Employment through civil-service examination rather than political connection is more firmly rooted in Los Angeles; that led earlier to a higher degree of professionalism within criminal-justice agencies than in other cities. For many years the Los Angeles police under Chief William Parker were considered the most professional force in the nation. It was less troubled by corruption; it was more thoroughly trained and better equipped than most other police departments. Its record keeping was more reliable. It was more fully isolated from political manipulation and control by the mayor, who in Los Angeles was much more a figurehead than a powerful executive. Therefore, it is not surprising that Los Angeles residents expressed a greater confidence in their police than did residents of other large cities.

The professionalism of the criminal-justice system is also illustrated by the way it handled the Watts riots in 1965. That uprising was the first of the series of major race riots that marked the mid-1960s and expressed the frustration of blacks at the slow improvement in their living conditions and life chances. In three days more than 3,000 arrests were made in Los Angeles, about ten times the normal number for a comparable period.[37] California law required that all persons arrested be arraigned within forty-eight hours of arrest or be released; a preliminary hearing had to be held within five days of the arraignment. In the first days when the riots were still proceeding or were a very vivid memory, court officials were under extraordinary pressure not to release arrested persons for fear that they would refuel the unrest. They set unusually high bail, and many of those arrested were not released until several days later. As time passed, it became clear, however, that many of the offenses were not terribly serious, that the evidence against the defendants was often shaky, and that it would be impossible to schedule trials for such a mass of defendants. Consequently, judges exerted strong pressure against defendants who insisted on a jury trial by levying very harsh penalties against those convicted; by contrast, persons pleading guilty received minimal sentences.[38] The result was that more persons were convicted than was ordinarily true, but fewer of those received convictions on felony charges or were given prison sentences.[39] As Isaac Balbus, one of the major critics of governmental responses to the riots, writes:

> Los Angeles court authorities had successfully "managed" the intense contradiction among their interests in order, formal rationality, and organizational maintenance which had been made manifest by what was at that time the single largest instance of collective violence in America in this century.... The bulk of over 3,000 cases were disposed of within four months following the revolt without either a serious disruption of the processing of "normal" criminal and civil cases or a wholesale, overt, and public abandonment of the standard legal norms entailed in formal rationality.[40]

Fragmentation of governmental services is the other characteristic of Los Angeles displayed prominently in the criminal-justice system. Los Angeles has a strong city council, a weak mayor, and many departments run by commissions rather than by the mayor. City elections are almost uninfluenced by political parties. Moreover, the city must share many powers with the county, which has its own fragmented governmental structure. As a result, there is no dominant force to direct public policy in Los Angeles. The police, for instance, are not under the effective control of the mayor. Formally, the mayor appoints the police commission, which in turn appoints the chief of police. But the mayor can make appointments only with the consent of the city council and can remove commissioners only with its consent. Los Angeles mayors rarely control the council through party connections; rather, they must learn to coexist with the council and maintain support through shifting coalitions. Consequently, the police commission enjoys a considerable degree of autonomy. Moreover, the chief of police has traditionally had a powerful voice; his authority has sometimes rivaled the mayor's. Unlike the situation in Chicago and New York, Los Angeles mayors cannot expect the chief of police to do their bidding.

Los Angeles courts and the prosecutor's office are organized on a countywide basis, as they are in Chicago, but they are not integrated with city politics through a political organization. Rather, they tend to go their own way, making the administration of criminal justice in Los Angeles County highly variable. For instance, 24 percent of those convicted of robbery in Los Angeles were sent to prison, but a few miles away in Long Beach, 30 percent received a prison sentence. For assault, the proportion of convicted persons sent to prison ranged from 1 percent in Pomona to 11 percent in Norwalk, with Los Angeles having a rate of 8 percent.[41] These variations existed at all stages of the felony disposition process. They also occurred within the city of Los Angeles with one judge sending 7 percent of the robbers convicted in his courtroom to prison and another sending 57 percent.[42] Such variations are not unique to Los Angeles; they exist in many metropolitan areas where the prosecutor's office and the courts extend over both the central city and many suburbs. Los Angeles is more typical than Chicago because most metropolitan areas lack informal mechanisms for coordinating the separate governmental bodies. The result is a much higher degree of variability in the administration of criminal justice in an area like Los Angeles.

The contrast between Los Angeles and Chicago illustrates one of the dilemmas facing designers of criminal-justice systems. The high degree of professionalism in each of the Los Angeles criminal-justice agencies promotes autonomy. Each agency responds to its own professional or occupational reference group. The police take their standards from police organizations; the prosecutor and public defender think in terms of norms established by the American Bar Association and by the specialized associations of prosecutors and public defenders. Judges evaluate themselves in terms of the criteria established by the judiciary. None of these groups considers the demands of political leaders legitimate within their area of expertise. Thus, popular influence remains remote in the operation of the criminal-justice system, and strong leadership by a single executive is equally difficult. The separate agencies may be swept along a joint course by a common tide, but often each agency responds to its own needs rather than to a common vision of the public good.

prairie city

Most urban Americans live in cities with populations under 250,000. These are the smaller cities and towns of the mythical middle America. Many of them are satellites of larger central cities in metropolitan areas: the Belmonts in Massachusetts and California, Skokie

outside Chicago, Monroe outside Pittsburgh, Metarie outside New Or-
leans, or Santa Monica outside Los Angeles. But many others are independent cities, centers of industry and commerce: the Springfields
in Massachusetts, Illinois, and Missouri; Grand Rapids, Michigan; or
Greensboro, North Carolina.

While we tend to associate crime with the largest cities, it is, as
we saw in chapter 2, also a severe problem in the smaller cities. We
know less about the incidence of crime in each of these places or
about the operation of their criminal-justice agencies. Some studies do
exist, however, suggesting the principal characteristics of crime and
justice in smaller cities.

As we saw in chapter 2, crimes of violence occur somewhat less
frequently in small cities than in the larger ones, but property crimes
are more frequent. As in the remainder of the nation, crime rates have
risen steeply since 1960 and the public's awareness of crime as a severe problem has sharpened.

Several elements, however, distinguish criminal justice in
smaller and larger cities. Both crime and justice tend to be more visible; the officials who deal with them are more widely known. The bar
is smaller and more tightly knit. Small cities are more homogeneous,
and minority groups are less likely to be well organized or influential
in local politics.

Crime and justice are more visible in smaller cities. So many
crimes occur every day in New York, Chicago, and Los Angeles that
the media report only the most spectacular ones. Even those are
everyday occurrences; the public can scarcely distinguish today's
murders from yesterday's or the day before yesterday's. Not so in
smaller cities. Take, for example, Prairie City, a pseudonym for a city
several social scientists have studied. Homicides increased from two
in 1960 to seven in 1976, but they were still unusual enough to become the focus of speculation, gossip, and conversation for many
weeks. Small-city newspapers have a daily column printing the police
blotter; it reports every disturbance, each crime, and all arrests. Many
people read that report and recognize the names and places it men-
tions. Not so in Chicago or the other large cities. Such a column would
fill the entire newspaper, and only a small percentage of the readers
would have any connection with the names and places mentioned.

In smaller cities victims and offenders are not just names but
vaguely familiar faces. They are attached to other acquaintances, to
past incidents, and to distant relationships. Crimes are not impersonal
events; for many people they are small tragedies with which they can

empathize. Many crimes, of course, are passed off as the work of "bad elements" or of "people who live on the wrong side of the tracks," but even they are known and recognized. Crime and the punishments meted out to offenders are much less anonymous in smaller cities than in the largest ones.

Lawyers and criminal-justice officials also constitute a much more cohesive group in small cities. This does not mean that everyone cooperates or that a coordinated policy exists. It means that everyone dealing with crime knows almost everyone else in other positions on a first-name basis. They are likely to have worked together before and to recognize that they probably will do so again.

Lawyers in small cities are less specialized than in the large cities. No lawyers make their entire living from defending criminals. Those lawyers who defend many criminal cases are likely to make most of their living from serving individual clients in many other ways as well. For instance, in Prairie City regular defense lawyers tried two to four criminal cases per month.[43] While "elite" lawyers did not take criminal cases, 60 percent of the attorneys rated "high" on the status scale reported spending some time in criminal defense work.[44] Thus, many prominent lawyers who mostly handle wills, estates, and corporate matters also took occasional criminal cases. Moreover, in many small cities, assistant prosecutors are only part-time with the district attorney's office; they are likely to spend afternoons in a private civil practice. Many such towns also do not have a full-time public defender; rather, the county pays individual lawyers to defend indigents on a fee basis. Consequently, a much larger proportion of the bar in small cities has regular contact with the criminal-justice process than it does in Chicago or New York. More lawyers also depend on it to some degree for their living.

Lawyers also tend to know each other better. Prairie City had fewer than one hundred attorneys in private practice in the mid-1960s. The state attorney's office in Cook County (Chicago) had many more by itself. There were too many Prairie City attorneys for them to know each other intimately, but every lawyer was likely to know almost all the others at least by reputation. David Neubauer writes of Prairie City attorneys:

> Defense attorneys and the prosecutors respect their opposite number as competent counsel. . . . This crucial ingredient of mutual respect for one's opponent is reinforced by the continuity in personnel between defense and prosecution. Three of the five

dominant attorneys served as assistants to the present state's attorney. The two dominants who have not been prosecutors practiced criminal law for about fifteen years. Given the exchange in personnel and the long terms of several of the defense attorneys, it is obvious that working relations have developed. There are very few secrets. Each knows the other and knows what to expect from him. It is equally obvious that such continuing relationships can be premised only on respect and credibility. A lawyer can pull a fast one on his opponent once, but this would jeopardize his entire standing with the community.[45]

In addition, attorneys know the judges sitting in the local courts. In Prairie City, almost all attorneys appeared in court several times a year; none were purely office lawyers.[46] Moreover, the judges formerly were members of the little legal community working in Prairie City.

It is more difficult for a lawyer in Prairie City to play the role of maverick.[47] Lawyers who cooperate with the prosecutor and judge in processing cases will be rewarded with courtesies such as continuances when they need them, with compliments from the bench that may impress present or future clients, and with reasonableness in negotiating pleas. Lawyers who incur the anger of the judge or prosecutor might have a very unpleasant time practicing in court. The attorney cannot hope to work with another prosecutor because there are none and cannot shop for judges because there are no other judges. Indeed, attorneys have to appear before the same judges in civil matters where much larger fees are involved than in their criminal cases. Thus, judges and prosecutors in small cities tend to exercise closer control over the criminal-adjudication process than in large cities.

It should be no surprise that the result is a large number of guilty pleas. Trials are as unusual in small cities as in large ones. Penalties tend to be somewhat more severe, however, perhaps because crime is perceived as more aberrant in small cities than in large ones. The judges who hear criminal cases do not spend their entire time in criminal court but also hear civil cases and therefore do not become so accustomed to offenders as big-city judges. In smaller cities, judges are also less isolated from the community in which they live; they may perceive greater pressure for harsh sentences for those convicted of serious crimes.

Governmental institutions involved in the criminal-justice process are more likely to resemble those of Los Angeles than those of Chicago or New York. Most smaller cities are governed by officials elected on nonpatisan ballots; many have city-manager forms of government; few have meaningful party organizations. These characteristics seem to make a difference in the style of policing and in the work of the criminal-justice system. Unreformed cities—with partisan elections and political executives—are more likely to have a watchman style that emphasizes the maintenance of order; such cities have more arrests for disorderly conduct. Reformed cities, with highly professional city managers, emphasize legalistic or service policing styles and have many more drunkenness and intoxicated-driving arrests.[48]

In reformed cities, the police are likely to be relatively autonomous from elected officials, governed more by civil-service regulations than by directives from the mayor. City managers stand between the police and elected officials. Police officers are likely to be paid considerably less than in the large cities, however, and they are likely to have much less training. Thus, they are more likely to be city workers than trained professionals. The other agencies involved in criminal justice almost always are countywide; sometimes, they operate in several counties. That means that city officials have relatively little voice in their policy orientation or in the selection of their key personnel. Party does not bind city and county together as in Chicago, but they are not as uncoordinated as in Los Angeles.

How much police and prosecutors work together varies as much in smaller cities as in the larger ones. In Prairie City, the relationship was cool and distant, much affected by the differing perspectives of the two agencies. The police were more concerned with making arrests and could not understand why so many people they arrested were not successfully prosecuted. The state's attorney was more concerned with meeting legal requirements for conviction and was forced to go for misdemeanor convictions or dismissals in many instances.[49] In a study of four Wisconsin cities, severe conflict between the police and prosecutor's office was found in two; in another, the police chief worked for the defeat of the district attorney, but his detectives and the assistant prosecutors worked well together; and in the fourth there was no severe conflict between the two agencies.[50]

The formal division between agencies is, therefore, only sometimes bridged by informal cooperation. More often, the separate agencies of the criminal-justice system keep their distance from one another and respond to their separate imperatives. Thus, the police adopt the stance of either law-enforcers or peace-keepers with principal concern, however, for what happens on the street. Prosecutors and court personnel are less concerned with what happens on the street but must meet the legal criteria for conviction. These differences are the same as in large cities. They tend to be smoothed over by personal ties more often in small cities, but such personal relationships are not always sufficient to suppress conflict between the separate agencies, as the studies in Wisconsin and of Prairie City show.

conclusion

New York, Chicago, Los Angeles, and the smaller cities that have been studied do not represent urban America in a statistical sense. Yet they provide us with a glimpse of the variability of the criminal-justice process. Although each of these cities have the common elements we described in earlier chapters, each city has a distinctive configuration. In many cities the criminal-prosecution process is distinctive enough that attorneys from one city represent clients in another only at their own peril. If offenders were mobile and moved from one city to another in quick succession (which few do), they would soon recognize the idiosyncracies of each place they worked in. They would perceive that one city is lenient and another harsh, that one city has a slow process and another a speedy one, or that one city has police who can easily be bought off and another has an almost incorruptible force.

In no city is the criminal-justice process completely isolated from larger political forces. Even in cities like Los Angeles, the criminal-justice system bears the stamp of local politics at large—the lack of coordination, of a guiding executive, and of common policies. This is not a difference between large cities and small ones, but between cities with powerful political leadership and those with weak guidance.

Although much variety exists in the methods of coping with crime, no particular pattern commends itself as more effective or more just than another. Each of the cities we have described has a flawed criminal-justice system. The choice is not between error and perfection, but between the kind of flaw one chooses to live with.

notes

1 Federal Bureau of Investigation, *Uniform Crime Reports, 1976* (Washington, D.C.: Government Printing Office, 1977).

2 *New York Times*, February 24, 1967, p. 1.

3 *New York Times*, July 17, 1978, p. 1.

4 Law Enforcement Assistance Administration, *Criminal Victimization Surveys in Chicago, Detroit, Los Angeles, New York, and Philadelphia: A Comparison of 1972 and 1974 Findings* (Washington, D.C.: Government Printing Office, 1976), pp. 63, 67. The figures in the text exclude all personal theft as well as household larceny under $50 with an undetermined amount or attempted theft.

5 Ibid., p. 64.

6 Ibid., p. 65.

7 James Garofalo, *Public Opinion about Crime: The Attitudes of Victims and Nonvictims in Selected Cities* (Washington, D.C.: Government Printing Office, 1977), pp. 348–49.

8 Ibid., pp. 352–53.

9 Law Enforcement Assistance Administration, *Expenditure and Employment Data for the Criminal Justice System, 1976* (Washington, D.C.: Government Printing Office, 1978), p. 166.

10 *Chicago Tribune*, July 9, 1978, sec. 1, p. 14.

11 Peter Maas, *Serpico* (New York: Viking Press, 1973).

12 *The Knapp Commission Report on Police Corruption* (New York: George Braziller, 1972), pp. 2–3.

13 Ibid., p. 6.

14 Garofalo, *Public Opinion about Crime*, pp. 10, 357.

15 *New York Times*, July 17, 1978, p. B4.

16 Ibid.

17 Vera Institute of Justice, *Felony Arrests: Their Prosecution and Disposition in New York City's Courts* (New York: Vera Institute of Justice, 1977), p. 1.

18 *New York Times*, July 17, 1978, p. B1.

19 Ibid. for 1977 statistics; Vera Institute, *Felony Arrests*, p. 1, for 1971 statistics.

20 Ibid.

21 Maas, *Serpico*, p. 114.

22 Federal Bureau of Investigation, *Uniform Crime Reports, 1976*.

23 Richard Block, *Violent Crime* (Lexington, Mass.: Lexington Books, 1977), p. 54.

24 Ibid., pp. 54–55.

25 Ibid., p. 77.

26 Ibid.

27 Garofalo, *Public Opinion about Crime*, pp. 296–97.

28 Ibid., p. 306.

29 Law Enforcement Assistance Administration, *Expenditure and Employment Data*, pp. 88, 92.

30 *Chicago Tribune*, November 26, 1978, sec. 1, p. 10.

31 James Eisenstein and Herbert Jacob, *Felony Justice* (Boston, Mass.: Little, Brown and Company, 1977), pp. 98–125.

32 Federal Bureau of Investigation, *Uniform Crime Reports, 1976*.

33 Law Enforcement Assistance Administration, *Criminal Victimization*, pp. 47, 51.

34 Garofalo, *Public Opinion about Crime,* p. 331.

35 Ibid., pp. 332–33.

36 Ibid., pp. 309, 341, 357.

37 From *The Dialectics of Legal Repression: Black Rebels before the American Criminal Courts,* by Isaac D. Balbus, p. 84, © 1973 by the Russell Sage Foundation, New York.

38 Ibid., p. 71.

39 Ibid., pp. 73, 78, 82–83.

40 Ibid., p. 84.

41 Peter Greenwood and others, *Prosecution of Adult Felony Defendants in Los Angeles County: A Policy Perspective* (Santa Monica, Calif.: The Rand Corporation, 1973), p. 107.

42 Ibid., p. 111.

43 David W. Neubauer, *Criminal Justice in Middle America* (Morristown, N.J.: General Learning Press, 1974), p. 69.

44 Joel F. Handler, *The Lawyer and His Community* (Madison, Wis.: University of Wisconsin Press, 1967), p. 41.

45 Neubauer, *Criminal Justice in Middle America,* pp. 79–80. Copyright 1974 by General Learning Press. Reprinted by permission.

46 Handler, *The Lawyer and His Community,* p. 43.

47 Neubauer, *Criminal Justice in Middle America,* pp. 80–82.

48 James Q. Wilson, *Varieties of Police Behavior* (Cambridge, Mass.: Harvard University Press, 1968), pp. 274–75.

49 Neubauer, *Criminal Justice in Middle America,* pp. 54–63.

50 Neal A. Milner, *The Court and Local Law Enforcement* (Beverly Hills, Calif.: Sage Publications, 1971), pp. 115, 139, 168.

conflict,
the law,
and city
politics

Criminal acts are not the only incidents that embroil city residents in legal proceedings. Far more often they have conflicts with one another than can only or best be resolved through intervention by lawyers or courts. These are called civil disputes because the power of the government is not used principally to punish violators of legal norms; the police are rarely involved.

Civil courts often appear more remote from the urban political arena than criminal courts. The civil courts are a public facility more or less open to all who need their services. City politics may affect the conditions under which cities make courts available, and court decisions often have an important effect on city politics and life.

civil disputes

Three kinds of conflicts come into the civil courts. The largest number of disputes involve essentially private concerns of citizens about their family, their property, or their rights to public services. A second set of conflicts involves business concerns. These generally have an economic base and affect many persons at one time. A third set of disputes centers around governmental policies. Private citizens may sue the government in order to alter policy or the government may sue individuals, businesses, or other governmental agencies in order to carry out a public policy. These conflicts differ from those in the first set because the aim is to change policy affecting large numbers of people rather than to correct an individual grievance.

PRIVATE CONFLICTS

Private conflicts with legal ramifications are legion. Several categories account for many of them. The first involves marriage breakups. Every divorce requires legal action to nullify the marital relationship, which involves not only certifying that the marriage is over but also legitimizing the property settlement and custodial and financial arrangements for minor children. Where children are involved, divorce usually does not end the relationship between spouses; it puts it on a new basis. Visiting rights and support payments have to be specified, and means have to be provided for assuring that the agreement will be carried out. The ex-spouses are often no longer friends; they cannot count on their mutual regard to guarantee execution of the divorce agreement. A contract borne of conflict and disagreement is much more difficult to draft and execute than an agreement (such as a marriage contract) borne of love and mutual respect.

Many divorces, although simple and routine, involve the transfer of considerable money and important rights. They play an important role in setting the living conditions of many of a city's residents. In 1975, for instance, more than 1 million divorces occurred, producing 2 million newly divorced persons and putting 1 million children into broken homes.[1] In that year 3.7 percent of all American men and 5.3 percent of the women were counted among the divorced;[2] approximately 6 percent of all children were living with only one parent as the result of a divorce.[3] We have no information about the amount of alimony and child support initiated or paid in any given year, but if each divorce involves an average of only $1,000 per year, divorces annually generate more than $1 billion of transfer payments. As we shall see, divorce agreements are worked out privately with little public intervention. They have a substantial impact on public programs, however. Many divorced women are forced onto the welfare rolls when alimony and support payments prove insufficient to maintain them. Divorce produces problems for city schools and may increase the incidence of juvenile delinquency.

A second frequent private conflict with legal ramifications involves another relationship that is often long-term: landlord and tenant. There are frequent disagreements about the conditions of leases and about the circumstances under which the tenant may break them. Other conflicts arise about late rental payments and about improvements and repairs that tenants want from the landlord. Such disputes are most important to residents of rundown areas of cities, who have few alternative sources of housing. They potentially touch a large minority of city residents, however; in 1977 about 35 percent of all housing units in the United States were rented, most of them located within metropolitan areas.[4] Although only a few of the disputes between landlord and tenant become legal conflicts, they set the standards for the private settlement of most of the other disputes.

A third set of disputes involves private individuals and business concerns about consumer credit. Americans are addicted to credit cards and charge accounts. Many disputes arise over billings and late payments. Most are resolved privately, but a large number go to lawyers and courts for collections.

A fourth kind of private dispute arises between citizens and government agencies. This may involve welfare recipients and the agency from which they receive help; it may be a dispute between a property owner and the zoning board; it may pit the street department against residents who want potholes on their street filled. Since city agencies have become involved in many aspects of urban living, it is not surprising that some people have serious conflicts with them. Those conflicts are often resolved without the help of a lawyer and without going to court. But sometimes people resort to the law and sue the agency for what they believe is rightfully theirs. Such suits rarely involve policy matters; rather, they seek the resolution of essentially private disagreements between a resident and a public official.

A fifth common dispute involving private individuals arises from automobile accidents. In the states that do not have no-fault insurance, the person who is injured or whose car is damaged must collect from the driver who is at fault in the accident. The driver at fault is usually covered by an insurance company, and that company defends against the claim or eventually pays it. Automobile accidents, of course, are common in cities; they generate thousands of claims, which must be settled or adjudicated. As a result, billions of dollars are paid to compensate for injuries or damages. When there is no payment or too little, public facilities are often called upon to help the injured party—for instance, free medical attention in municipal hospitals or claims under the Medicaid provisions of welfare programs.

Table 7.1 shows the frequency of these five kinds of disputes in a national sample of the population. Over a lifetime, Americans appear to be more likely to suffer divorce than serious personal injury from an accident; they are more likely to have a dispute with a government agency than with a landlord. Property damage as the result of an accident is the most frequent source of problems. As the second column of table 7.1 indicates, the annual occurrence of these conflicts is much lower than that spread over a lifetime. But if we compare these rates with criminal victimization rates, we see that many of these kinds of civil disputes are much more common.

Such disputes are not distributed evenly among the population. Some people are much more prone to them than others. In a recent national survey whites were more likely to report serious property damage from accidents than blacks.[5] Whites were also much more likely to report problems with local agencies,[6] even though a larger proportion of blacks are on welfare programs, which one might expect to generate disputes. Divorces were reported by equal proportions of blacks and whites, but blacks reported being separated from their spouses much more often.[7] Blacks and Latinos were also more likely to report landlord-tenant problems.[8] In general, it appears that whites—especially those with good educations and substantial incomes—were more likely to make aggressive use of the law to settle disputes and that blacks, Latinos, and people who generally have little education or income were more often the objects of legal action.

Singly, none of these disputes or the other disagreements between individuals has much impact on city life or public policy. But

table 7.1
The Frequency of Private Disputes

type of dispute	number of adults who had problem at least once per 1,000 adults in population [a]	number of problems encountered each year per 1,000 adults in population [b]
Divorce	150	9
Eviction	40	3
Dispute with local agency	70	17
Serious personal injury	120	9
Serious property damage	400	68

[a] Barbara A. Curran, *Legal Needs of the Public* (Chicago, Ill.: American Bar Foundation, 1977), pp. 103–4. Reprinted by permission.

[b] Ibid., p. 171.

the cumulative effect is great. Not only is much money transferred as the result of settling these disputes, but city residents also develop a feeling that the legal system is treating them justly or unjustly. In a national sample more people with experience in the courts lacked confidence in them than people who had had no experience,[9] and almost as many with experience in civil courts reacted unfavorably toward them as favorably.[10] Among those familiar with state and local civil courts, only 1 percent rated them as excellent; 27 percent thought them fair or poor.[11] Thus, both direct experience with the civil courts as the result of private litigation and indirect knowledge of them from the media lead many people to rate them poorly. That is an important—if unintended—consequence of the way private disputes are adjudicated in civil courts.

BUSINESS DISPUTES

Business disputes typically concern contracts that one business contends another has broken—for instance, a contract for the delivery of goods or the construction of a new facility. The offended party usually seeks to settle the dispute privately because it wishes to maintain relations with the other firm or its associates. But even private settlement efforts involve lawyers and the legal system because settlements are usually made within the framework of what a court might possibly award as the result of a trial.

Another set of business disputes centers on labor relations. Much of the work force of large businesses is unionized and works under collective bargaining contracts that must be renewed periodically. The contracts also include provisions for settling grievances and disagreements about the execution of the agreements. Both negotiation of the contract and the settlement of grievances usually involve lawyers, but not the courts. One usually finds lawyers on the negotiating teams of both sides. Grievances are often settled privately or through arbitration proceedings, but these may also involve attorneys for both sides. Labor settlements have a decisive effect on a city's economy because they set the cost of labor, not only for unionized industries but also for nonunion firms that compete in the same market and for the city itself as an employer.

Because city employees have increasingly sought to gain the benefits of collective bargaining, the city often is a party to labor-management disputes. Whether they are the employers of sanitation workers, police, fire fighters, teachers, or clerical employees, cities find themselves forced to the bargaining table and sometimes are the object of strikes. In many states, strikes by public employees are illegal and can be stopped by obtaining a court injunction against them. Whether a mayor seeks an injunction rather than make further concessions to win a contract depends on the political strength of the union, the fiscal condition of the city, and other political ramifications of a strike or its settlement. In numerous cities, striking workers or their leaders have been hauled to jail because they refused to obey court orders to return to work; in many more, strikes have been avoided only after the intervention of labor lawyers who negotiated a settlement. In a few instances, settlements have been reached in a judge's chambers under the threat of an injunction.

Business cases and public employee negotiations typically involve large sums of money and have a significant impact on large numbers of people. In such disputes the legal system is used not only as a regulator of commerce to maintain the relationships and exchanges that characterize the commercial life of a city but also to set bounds for the relationship between the city and its employees.

POLICY DISPUTES WITH GOVERNMENT AGENCIES

The third kind of conflict directly involves governmental agencies in policy disputes. The conflict may arise from a charge that one business is "unfairly" competing with other firms and consequently an antitrust complaint is filed. Disputes over racial integration of schools have often landed in the courts. Disputes over zoning of land parcels and developers' plans for construction of new housing or commercial facilities frequently go to court. Conflicts between government officials about their jurisdiction and powers over each other and over the outcome of elections may also go to court for final adjudication.[12]

These kinds of conflict occur less frequently than private or business disputes, but higher stakes are involved because each individual case may affect the lives of thousands of city residents and sometimes the very future of the city itself. In many of these disputes the legal process is used as an instrument to formulate public policy or to obtain its implementation. A zoning dispute, for instance, may involve the future of an entire downtown area, or it may shape the demands that will be made of the city for providing services to outlying areas in future years. Some of these disputes involve city officials directly; others simply take place in the city and have their effects in other communities or in the local private sector. For instance, antitrust suits usually are brought in large commercial centers because the companies involved do their business there. But the outcome of such cases often has effects that range far more broadly than the city in which the case is settled or tried.

All of the disputes that we have described are thought of as civil disputes rather than criminal. In general, that means that the remedy sought is compensation rather than punishment, although "punitive damages" are sometimes awarded plaintiffs in civil cases. The most important procedural difference from criminal cases, however, is that those who have been injured or whose property has been damaged must usually pursue their claims on their own; no public official like the prosecuting attorney will take their place or act in their stead. If they need a lawyer—and most people do when they pursue a civil action—they must get their own. The conditions under which attorneys process these kinds of claims and others, therefore, are especially important in understanding the role of civil litigation in city politics.

the urban bar

Because most people who have civil disputes must use a lawyer, attorneys function as gatekeepers to the civil courts. They determine in the first instance whether the dispute is worth pursuing and then whether it can be settled out of court or whether a formal court proceeding is necessary. The benefits people derive from legal proceedings depend a great deal on whether they go to an attorney and what kind of attorney they find to represent them.

Attorneys occupy their gatekeeping position because they have the special knowledge and connections required to resolve legal disputes. Their knowledge is arcane; they know or can research the pertinent laws. They know which courts to go to if that action becomes necessary and how to proceed in them. Although an individual may legally take his or her own case to court, no one but a lawyer may represent him or her in court. Taking one's own case to court is usually foolish because nonlawyers do not know all the technicalities that may defeat them. In addition to this special knowledge, lawyers also have the connections that are useful or necessary to settle the dispute. They often have worked with the attorneys representing the other side and know how to approach them. They often know whom to contact in a large firm or government agency. They generally receive better treatment in court; for instance, their cases are called before those of unrepresented litigants.

When facing problems with legal ramifications, people have several choices. They may simply avoid the conflict by accepting defeat; for instance, when evicted they may prefer flight to fight when that is the cheaper alternative. In fact, about half the persons who face eviction choose the no-action alternative.[13] But people do something about most of the problems that confront them. Problems with creditors, wage garnishments, and disputes with federal, state, or local agencies are among those that elicit a response in 90 percent or more of the cases.[14]

A person's response, however, need not be to run to a lawyer. In many instances people rely on other resources. They may simply go to the other party by themselves and work out their own settlement. For instance, in many consumer disputes people contact manufacturers or the Better Business Bureau. In landlord-tenant disputes, people who do not go to a lawyer are likely to turn to elected officials to help them settle the dispute.[15] Elected officials are even more prominent dispute referees when the conflict involves a government agency.

Several kinds of problems, however, frequently bring people to lawyers. If they seek help at all, they are likely to go to a lawyer when they face eviction, when they have suffered a personal injury from an accident, and when they have a dispute with a local regulatory agency. As table 7.2 shows, a substantial proportion of all persons who seek help go to lawyers in these cases. In addition, divorces usually involve lawyers.

Lawyers are not obligated to represent all potential litigants. Indeed, they have the duty of dissuading disputants from going to court if it appears that they have no legal basis for their claims. Simple

table 7.2
Use of Lawyers in Civil Disputes

disputes	percentage of those who used a resource who used a lawyer
Eviction	69%
Personal injury	56%
Dispute with local agency	43%

Source: Barbara A. Curran, *Legal Needs of the Public* (Chicago, Ill.: American Bar Foundation, 1977), p. 139. Reprinted by permission.

economics, moreover, usually dictate that lawyers will not accept persons as clients unless the case can pay. Personal-injury suits are usually accepted on a contingent-fee basis. If the lawyer wins compensation for the client, he or she is paid a percentage of the settlement; if no compensation results, the lawyer is paid nothing. Thus, lawyers often reject cases that are unlikely to result in payment of a claim. Most other kinds of cases are taken on the basis of a specific fee or retainer. If the potential fee that the attorney quotes is greater than the amount of compensation that might be won, most clients will find some other way of settling the dispute—often by simply forgetting about it or turning to another dispute-settling process.

Hence, lawyers operate as gatekeepers to the legal system. They agree to represent some clients because it is profitable; others they turn away. Some segments of a city's population are much more likely to be served than others. Blacks and Latinos have lawyers much less frequently than whites. The rate for blacks and Latinos was 250 per 1,000 occurrences of a legal problem, and for whites it was 320 per 1,000.[16] The difference is most marked with respect to marital problems and disputes with government agencies. There are other problems on which minorities use lawyers more often than whites; this is true for torts (personal-injury cases), where whites more frequently negotiate settlements on their own. Likewise, when faced with eviction, blacks use lawyers at a rate of 520 per 1,000 occurrences as compared to the white rate of 180 per 1,000. The difference results from the fact that 59 percent of the whites when threatened with eviction simply moved away, whereas only 17 percent of the blacks and Latinos did so.[17] In addition, persons with high incomes generally use lawyers more often than those with lower incomes except for tort cases, where low-income persons use lawyers more often.[18] Finally, women are more likely to use attorneys than men, especially in divorce cases where by custom they are usually the plaintiff.[19]

Not all clients use the same kind of lawyers. Which lawyers they use and how well they are served depends on the size of the city and on the structure of its legal profession.

The legal profession in most American cities is stratified. At the top sit the attorneys working in large firms. Somewhat lower in the scale are attorneys working in smaller firms. At the bottom are lawyers who simply share offices with other attorneys but who essentially work by themselves as solo practitioners. This stratification is most sharply defined in large cities. In smaller towns, the distinctions between the groups are blurred.[20]

The distinctions among these three types of lawyers rest on several differences between attorneys that have a cumulative effect. First, lawyers in large firms tend to come from more socially prominent families than solo practitioners. The scions of important business executives are recruited for the large firms; the sons of immigrant and ethnic-minority families tend to go into small firms and solo work. This occurs in part because the large firms seek the business connections that the sons and daughters of prominent families bring with them. But it is also the result of the kind of education that children of such families enjoy. Upper-class children tend to go to prestigious universities and law schools. If they do well, they have a much better chance of being recruited by a large law firm than if they did well in a middle-range or mediocre law school. For instance, the Wall Street firms of New York recruit largely at Columbia, Harvard, Yale, Cornell, and Pennsylvania. Graduates of the SUNY-Buffalo law school have less of a chance at these jobs. La Salle Street firms in Chicago recruit mostly at the University of Chicago, Northwestern, and Michigan; graduates of Loyola, DePaul, or Kent have much less chance to win a job at these firms.

It is not, however, the higher status of the incoming lawyers that puts large firms at the top of the stratification scale. The large firms are on the top because they represent the most prestigious clients and handle the most intellectually challenging problems. The prestige of clients rubs off onto the lawyers representing them. Consequently, attorneys representing the biggest corporations and the wealthiest individuals in a city have the highest prestige; those representing the poor are generally at the bottom of the heap.[21]

The large firms also handle the most complicated legal problems, which involve securities transactions, tax matters, banking affairs, and antitrust actions. Lawyers consider these much more complex and challenging than personal injury, divorce, landlord-tenant, or general family affairs, the sorts of problems that individuals bring to solo lawyers or small firms.

In addition, partners in the large firms generally earn the highest incomes. They typically command incomes of more than $100,000 a year; partners of smaller firms usually earn between $30,000 and $80,000. Solo practitioners most frequently earn the lowest incomes among lawyers, with some earning less than $15,000 annually.[22]

Lawyers in these three milieu operate quite differently. There are two kinds of lawyers in law firms: the young attorney (called an associate), who works on a salary; and the partner, who shares in the firm's profits. Solo practitioners live solely off their fees, and there is a fairly close relationship between the work they do for particular clients and their earnings.

Relationships with clients differ sharply among the three types of lawyers. The large- and middle-sized firms have long-standing relationships with clients who bring them large amounts of business. Lawyers in these circumstances get to know a great deal about their clients' affairs. It is rare for a single client to control such a large portion of a firm's work that the client can influence the law firm by threatening to go to another firm. Rather, the law firm and client develop a close relationship that directly benefits the firm because it can count on a steady source of income from the work sent it by its business clients. At the other end of the stratification scale, solo practitioners and those who share offices with a couple of other lawyers have fleeting relationships with dozens of clients. Many of their clients are walk-ins who come to them almost by chance—through a mutual acquaintance, because their office is in the neighborhood, because they belong to the same club or church as the lawyer. Such clients typically come for one problem and return only after a long interval, if at all.[23] Each action nets the practitioner only a small fee; he or she needs many such clients to make a living. No single client commands the solo practitioner's attention.

The large firms are more specialized and have attorneys in subspecialties. For instance, a half dozen large firms in Chicago are known for their work in defending business corporations in antitrust cases. Each firm has attorneys who have become expert in certain industries or with respect to certain economic matters. These firms also have small estate and tax divisions, but that is not the main thrust of their work. Such firms do not advertise their specialty. They do not need to; business corporations know about them by their reputation. Smaller law firms are less specialized and typically handle a wider range of matters; they may handle an occasional antitrust case for a small corporation and do much tax, estate, merger, and contract work. Solo practitioners are usually the least specialized. They handle almost any case brought by the clients who walk into their offices. They will take criminal matters if they must, as well as divorces, individual tax returns, estates, real estate transactions, and any of the other matters affecting individuals and small businesses. Because they work alone, they cannot easily consult with a more specialized lawyer. While the attorney in a large firm can call in a specialist from across the hall when confronted with a complicated matter in a field he or she does not know well, the solo practitioner generally struggles with the problem alone. Consequently, the clients of large firms often receive much more expert advice than clients of small firms and of solo practitioners.

The amount of stratification and specialization is much greater in large cities than in small ones. The smaller the city, the more its lawyers have a general practice in which they represent both business firms and individuals and handle both corporate and personal matters. Although even middle-sized cities have law firms with as many as a dozen partners, they are not very far removed in status from solo practitioners in such cities. Unlike solo practitioners in big cities, small town solo practitioners may have almost as much prestige as the partners of the largest law firm; they may make almost the same income; and they may be handling many of the same kinds of legal problems.[24]

provision of legal services

The legal profession is especially well organized to handle the disputes that involve large sums of money and important clients. The large law firms spring to action in such cases; they bring their considerable expertise to these problems. The litigants often have long-standing relationships with law firms that know their affairs intimately.

Not so for the common citizen. Recent surveys indicate that many people have legal problems that they do not bring to their lawyers.[25] This is the result of many factors. Most people do not know a lawyer and do not know where they can find reliable legal advice. Although some advertising by lawyers is now permitted, it remains uncommon. Compare, for instance, the telephone yellow pages for lawyers and doctors. When looking for a physician, a person can find both the names of all physicians in the area and also their specialties. The potential patient is unlikely to wander into the waiting room of a psychiatrist when he needs an opthamologist. That is not true for lawyers. Although many lawyers have informal specialties, few are certified; it is rare to find a listing of specialists in the telephone directory. So, the ordinary person is likely to stumble into the office of a divorce lawyer when he wants to buy a house or into the anteroom of a personal-injury lawyer when he needs tax advice.

In addition, the lawyers who handle personal matters are often less specialized than their large-firm counterparts. Consequently, the ordinary person usually obtains less expert legal advice, not simply because he or she went to the wrong specialist but because the attorney who has agreed to handle the case generally has less expert knowledge.

Many persons with legal problems get beyond the obstacle raised by their failure to know a lawyer. Most cities have lawyers' referral services run by the local bar association. The referral service will give the name of an attorney who might be willing to take the case and who will give an initial interview for a stated, nominal fee. But other deterrents to using lawyers arise. Many people fear, often unrealistically, that legal fees will be too high. But lawyers' fees may be substantial and often cannot be stated precisely until the dispute is settled or dropped because the amount of time a lawyer puts into the matter, which is the basis for the fee, cannot be accurately predicted.

These problems are widespread among the population. For instance, 83 percent of a national sample agreed with the statement that many people do not go to lawyers "because they had no way of knowing which lawyer is competent to handle their particular problem."[26] Sixty-eight percent thought lawyers cost more than they were worth.[27] Those persons who had used lawyers did not have substantially better opinions about these matters than those who never had. Nor were there substantial differences on these matters by race.[28] Thus, public perceptions of the legal profession keep many people from using the services of lawyers.

Not all persons are equally turned back, however. The likelihood of seeing an attorney about a legal problem varies with income and race. In Detroit, for instance, persons with higher incomes who had personal legal problems were more likely to use a lawyer than persons with lower incomes.[29] Likewise, whites were much more likely to go to a lawyer with any given problem than were blacks.[30] The difference between the number of people who reported problems and those who indicated that they saw a lawyer about them was dramatic. For instance, only 4 percent of the whites reporting discrimination (usually on the basis of sex or age) and 7 percent of the blacks went to a lawyer in Detroit.[31]

To overcome some of these problems of unmet legal needs, new forms of legal organization have been established in most cities. These are legal-service offices located in neighborhoods to provide assistance for persons with low incomes. Most of the money for these offices comes from the federal government; the lawyers work for the legal-service organization rather than for individual clients. Many of these offices are located in storefronts. They provide help mostly in routine private disputes involving family matters, landlord-tenant conflicts, disputes with merchants and lenders, and the like. They rarely handle personal-injury cases since those can be sent to other lawyers who will take them on a contingent-fee basis. Although hundreds of thousands of cases are handled by these offices each year, it is still estimated that legal-service offices meet only half the needs of low-income persons.[32]

Such offices are no help to persons with modest incomes, such as the ordinary working family with sufficient income to meet daily expenses but not enough to afford what they think may be an expensive lawyer. To meet their needs, individual lawyers have increasingly organized themselves into neighborhood legal clinics. Using paraprofessionals for routine work and advertising standard fees for routine matters, such offices bring legal services closer to the people who need them and offer somewhat greater expertise than the ordinary solo practitioner.

Nevertheless, the most recent studies indicate that a large portion of the legal needs of the ordinary person are not met. This has particularly important consequences when the person is a defendant in a case brought by a large organization that is well represented. For instance, in debt collection cases lenders are routinely represented by collection firms that specialize in collecting debts; they go to court and often win default judgments against the debtor because the debtor did not know enough to come to court to defend himself or herself. With judgment in hand, the creditor then can call upon the sheriff to seize part of the debtor's wages (called wage garnishment), to recover the car or household appliance that was bought on a conditional sales contract, or to evict the tenant from his or her home. The consequences of not being represented in such actions are disastrous.

Because of the structure of the legal profession, the legal services provided in most cities are skewed. Although the courts in theory are open to everyone and although the laws are written as if everyone can use the remedies they make available, certain classes within the city are able to take much better advantage of these facilities and remedies than others. Consequently, civil courtrooms are much more the domain of the business community and propertied individuals than of the poor. The reason is that lawyers are better organized to serve business corporations and wealthy individuals than ordinary people with ordinary problems. Ordinary people are often screened out of the legal process—first, by their difficulty in finding legal assistance; second, by the reluctance of lawyers to take small cases; and third, by the marginal competence of attorneys to handle private cases when they do take them.

conclusion

City residents have a wide range of disputes that sometimes come to the legal arena for settlement. Many of these disputes are private; they do not directly involve public policy although their cumulative effect may be very substantial. In the aggregate, billions of dollars are transferred as the result of such private disputes; they mold the lives of a very large segment of the city's population.

Whether a dispute reaches the legal arena, however, depends on the structure of the city's legal profession. It depends on whether appropriate forms of legal organizations exist to provide services. Moreover, the quality of the service depends on the ability to pay.

Civil disputes are handled in ways both similar to and different from criminal matters. In civil cases lawyers occupy a mediating position much like the role of the police with the crime problem. The police decide whether an incident is a crime; their activities are required to set the criminal prosecution process into motion. Likewise, lawyers determine whether a problem is appropriate for civil remedies. The lawyer has even more discretion in handling potential civil matters than a police officer does in deciding about crime.

There are substantial differences from the city's handling of the crime problem. Most important is how little government is involved in screening civil disputes. The bar is a private enterprise in most instances; government-funded legal services provide only a small portion of all the legal services the public uses. Consequently, city officials play a minor role in determining the quality of legal assistance for their residents. How much people get is more the result of the marketplace than of governmental policy.

Moreover, more social classes are involved in civil disputes than in criminal matters. Crime, as we saw, is concentrated among the poor; civil disputes occur among all strata of the population. Nevertheless, the legal problems of all segments of the population are not treated equally. The legal profession is structured so that it provides better services for the affluent than for the poor.

Cities are not entirely passive with respect to providing civil justice for their residents. Courts play an important role in determining the pattern of outcomes, as we shall see in the next chapter.

notes

1 U.S. Department of Commerce, *Statistical Abstract of the United States, 1977* (Washington, D.C.: Government Printing Office, 1977), table 97.

2 Ibid., table 45.

3 Ibid., table 60.

4 Ibid., table 1,271.

5 Barbara A. Curran, *The Legal Needs of the Public* (Chicago, Ill.: American Bar Foundation, 1977), p. 118.

6 Ibid., p.115.

7 Ibid., p. 114.

8 Ibid., p. 109.

9 Yankelovich, Skelly and White, Inc., *The Public Image of Courts* (Williamsburg, Va.: National Center for State Courts, 1978), p. 17.

10 Ibid., p. 18.

11 Ibid., p. 24.

12 Kenneth M. Dolbeare, *Trial Courts in Urban Politics* (New York: John Wiley & Sons, 1967), pp. 34–36.

13 Curran, *Legal Needs of the Public*, p. 38.

14 Ibid., p. 137.

15 Ibid., p. 140.

16 Ibid., p. 149.

17 Ibid., p. 151.

18 Ibid., p. 153.

19 Ibid., p. 147.

20 Edward O. Laumann and John P. Heinz, "Specialization and Prestige in the Legal Profession: The Structure of Deference," *American Bar Foundation Research Journal* (1977), pp. 155–216, describe the situation in a big city. For small towns, see Joel Handler, *The Lawyer and His Community* (Madison: University of Wisconsin Press, 1967).

21 Laumann and Heinz, "Specialization and Prestige."

22 John P. Heinz and others, "Diversity, Representation, and Leadership in an Urban Bar: A First Report of a Survey of the Chicago Bar," *American Bar Foundation Research Journal* (1967), p. 727; *New York Times*, May 16, 1977, p. 35.

23 Jerome Carlin, *Lawyers on Their Own* (New Brunswick, N.J.: Rutgers University Press, 1962).

24 Handler, *The Lawyer and His Community*.

25 Curran, *Legal Needs of the Public*, pp. 134–84.

26 Ibid., p. 228.

27 Ibid., p. 231.

28 Ibid., pp. 235, 248.

29 Leon Mayhew and Albert J. Reiss, "The Social Organization of Legal Contacts," *American Sociological Review*, 34 (1969), 314.

30 Ibid., p. 313.

31 Ibid., p. 316.

32 Harry P. Stumpf, "Law and Poverty: A Political Perspective," *Wisconsin Law Review* (1968), p. 700; statement by Thomas Ehrlich at hearings before Subcommittee of the House Appropriations Committee, 2d Supplemental Appropriation Bill, 1976, 94th Congress, 2d Session, p. 88.

*dispute
processing
in american
cities*

*d*isputes are processed in several distinct ways. In some, lawyers play an important role; in others, their influence is marginal or absent. Some involve the public institutions of the city in a central way; others are simply allowed to flourish, without direct public involvement.

The four most important means of processing disputes are avoidance, negotiation, mediation, and adjudication. Avoidance is simply escape; people run from their problems and declare them no longer pertinent to their lives. Negotiation involves explicit bargaining between the parties involved and a settlement agreeable to both. Mediation also involves bargaining but under the aegis of a third party whom both disputants accept and respect. Adjudication involves the imposition of a settlement by an authoritative third party after a formal proceeding that establishes the facts and determines which rules are pertinent to settling the case. Adjudication occurs most prominently in courts; it is the means of dispute processing most readily manipulated by government. We will discuss the processes separately, but we need to remember that each is affected by the presence and operation of the others.

avoidance

Escape and avoidance may well be the most common process for "settling" disputes in the United States.[1] People run away from their conflicts because the benefit of pursuing justice may be too small, because the costs of obtaining a more favorable result may be too high, or because their circumstances may permit easy escape. Each of these conditions applies differently to different sets of people depending on their circumstances.

We saw in the previous chapter that most whites who face eviction simply leave, while most blacks resist in some form. Such a differential response to the threat of losing one's residence probably results from different opportunities to escape. Whites, even when poor, have many more options in the housing market than blacks. They can more readily move to a different neighborhood and apparently do so. Likewise, we noted that while divorce rates are somewhat lower for blacks than whites, separation is more frequent for blacks. The reason is that divorce requires formal action and is usually more costly; desertion has long been the poor man's alternative to divorce. While most whites are able to afford negotiations and adjudication to obtain a divorce, many blacks use the avoidance technique of separation or desertion.

In addition, the benefits of pursuing another solution to one's problems may be too slight to make it worthwhile, For instance, if one suffers minor property damage as the result of an auto accident, it may not be worth running after the other party even if he or she is entirely at fault because the effort expended is not worth the ultimate payment that might result. Likewise, if one feels that a supermarket has sold poor goods, it is easier to take one's trade to a competitor than to pursue the complaint in order to get a refund. If one feels that a physician is not giving good enough care to one's family, it is easier to switch doctors than to complain to the local medical society. Thus, numerous occasions dictate avoidance rather than any other action.

How attractive avoidance is depends particularly on whether alternatives are available. Consequently, cities can affect the rate at which people faced with eviction notices move rather than contest the landlord's action by supplying alternative housing or by making housing courts more or less readily accessible. Cities can develop alternative institutions for processing disputes that make avoidance less attractive. But where alternative institutions and processes do not exist, many people will find it more economical to accept the loss imposed by the dispute rather than contest it.

negotiation

Negotiated settlement is a common alternative to avoidance. Escape may be too costly because the parties want or need to continue to interact. Just as running away from home is not feasible for most children, pulling up stakes and moving a business is not possible for most business people. Many disputes occur within the framework of generally acceptable and mutually profitable relationships. A firm, for instance, may have a dispute about one shipment but runs into no trouble at all with a host of others to the same customer. One may be generally satisfied with purchases at a store despite a single bad experience. One may want to continue renting one's apartment despite a conflict with the landlord over his obligation to paint the hallways. Thus, the first prerequisite of negotiations is that all parties must be willing to settle the dispute.[2]

Negotiation also requires that the parties find a place where they can negotiate. Sometimes the site is a neutral location, since going to the residence or work place of one or the other party gives (or seems to give) that side an undue advantage. At other times the site is a culturally accepted location such as a complaint desk at a store even though it is located on the turf of one of the parties to the dispute. Law offices are frequently the site of negotiations in the United States.

Negotiations proceed by defining the issues and exchanging maximum and minimum claims. Once the parties have agreed upon the issues and stated the limits of their demands and concessions, they bargain until they conclude the dispute. The particular bargain that is struck depends on the strength of each side and the costs each is willing to bear to continue the relationship. It also depends on the likelihood that one side will lapse into avoidance or, alternatively, go to adjudication. The costs and benefits of alternative processes are constantly implicit in negotiations.

In the United States, most negotiations are entirely private and are affected by city policies only in so far as those policies provide alternatives. Most consumer complaints are settled either by avoidance or by negotiation, because cities have typically not provided viable alternatives. Were consumer affairs agencies established that provided inexpensive mediation or adjudication of consumer disputes, many more disputes would probably end up there, and the complaint desks at stores would probably see fewer cases. Some negotiations take place within the context of formal adjudication procedures. For instance, most divorce decrees are negotiated before they are presented to the court for final adjudication. In the typical divorce case,

148

the lawyer for the wife, who usually is the complainant, gets together with the attorney for the husband to work out the details of property settlement, alimony, and child support and custody. These are typically negotiated without any third-party intervention although the negotiations are usually conducted by representatives of the couple rather than by the husband and wife themselves. These representatives typically have considerable knowledge about the normal arrangements that meet the standards of the law and the expectations of the community. Consequently, they produce settlements that divorce courts can readily endorse. Many personal-injury suits are also settled out of court, often with no intervention by the court, although the threat of formal adjudication usually hangs over the settlement process.[3]

Negotiations are the particular hallmark of business disputes. A city's legal community plays a prominent role in processing disputes through negotiation. The large law firms of big cities and the most prominent lawyers in small cities spend much of their time negotiating settlements between business adversaries. Some of these negotiators play quite specialized roles. For instance, labor negotiators work only for labor unions and management representatives handle only the firm's side. In other kinds of disputes a law firm is likely to work for a wide variety of clients.

mediation and arbitration

Mediation and arbitration involve third parties. Mediation is a process by which a third party who is mutually agreeable to the disputants seeks to bring them to a settlement. It resembles negotiations, except for the active involvement of a third party. Arbitration carries the process one step closer to imposed judgments. The parties agree in advance to accept the decision of the arbitrator whom they themselves choose.

Both mediation and arbitration require a social setting in which disputants can find mutually acceptable third parties. That means that their lives must intersect in such a way that they share some fundamental values and contacts. Alternatively, formal institutions must exist that, although impersonal, have won respect and trust from disputants for their neutrality. The first condition frequently does not exist in American cities. Americans lead rather isolated lives in their cities. They may or may not know their neighbors; the people with whom they work are likely to live in quite different areas and come from different ethnic and religious backgrounds. They are unlikely to have extended family relationships in their immediate vicinity. Some institutions have been established to provide equivalent services, however. The federal government has a mediation service to help settle labor disputes; the American Arbitration Association is a private nationwide organization that supplies arbitrators for almost any kind of dispute brought to it.

Cities have not been very active in developing mediation services for their citizens, although some do exist. A few cities have neighborhood justice centers that provide such services.[4] In addition, some cities have ombudsmen for particular agencies, whose job it is to handle complaints and mediate between the citizen and the agency. Likewise, some newspapers provide an "action line" service that mediates disputes between private parties and between citizens and government agencies.[5]

adjudication

Court action takes place within the context of these other alternatives. It is usually, but not always, the last resort. It is the dispute process most subject to city control because it is a governmental function. Adjudication in the courts resolves disputes by authoritative decisions handed down by judges who examine the facts and apply the pertinent law. The judge's decision is binding; the force of the state can be invoked to execute it.

Cities have a wide variety of judicial institutions to handle civil disputes. In some cities civil courts are the same institutions as the criminal courts. The judges are the same; the clerks are the same; the courtrooms and other physical facilities are the same. Only the rules by which litigation is processed and sometimes the attorneys are different. In other cities entirely different sets of personnel handle civil disputes. Generally the smaller the city, the more likely it is that the same court handles both criminal and civil cases. Even many large cities use the same judges for both courts, although the courtrooms tend to be specialized. In these cities, judges rotate through the various specialized courtrooms, working for a while in a criminal court, moving to divorce court, going to a courtroom hearing jury trials of personal-injury cases, moving to another courtroom to hear evictions, sitting in probate court, and eventually returning to the criminal court.[6]

Except where judges' assignments are permanent or very long, judges are the least expert members of the courtroom team in civil cases. Attorneys, unlike judges, tend to specialize in particular kinds of litigation and become expert in the work of a particular court over the course of their career. Unlike the criminal court, however, no attorney is permanently assigned to a particular courtroom. None works for the government in the same way the prosecutor does in criminal proceedings. Instead, all attorneys are private or represent a particular government agency. All of them are occasional members of the courtroom team, but in a few courts some appear with great regularity.

Civil-court proceedings are often much more formal than the other modes of dispute processing. They require considerably greater resources. To initiate a case, a disputant must make a formal complaint that is filed with the court and transmitted to the defendant. The complainant must allege some wrong that the court has the power to correct. The defendant is then given time to respond to the charges. He or she may do so by denying the wrong, by asserting that the court has no power to intervene, or by claiming that he or she is the party that has been wronged and therefore should benefit from whatever remedy the court may dispense. After all the claims and counter-claims have been filed, the case is ready for the court to begin its processing. That occurs through motions made before the court for collecting evidence (subpoenas and depositions), for disclosing evidence (discovery), and for rulings on the legal foundation of the complaints. In simple cases these preliminaries are avoided; in more complicated matters they may take years by themselves. After all these preliminaries have been completed, the case is ready for trial when the court finds the time to hear it.

Before the case is scheduled for trial, however, most courts handling major disputes require litigants to attend a pretrial conference at which several matters are discussed, often with the judge present. First, attorneys are asked to come to an agreement about elements of the evidence that are not disputed. The agreement saves much time at the trial since such evidence can simply be stipulated for the record rather than entered through testimony. Second, attorneys are asked to agree to the legal issues on which they concede there is no conflict and to pinpoint those on which they disagree. Both of these activies sharpen the issues remaining in conflict and may make clear the likely outcome of the trial. Consequently, a third function of the pretrial conference is to seek an agreement that will avoid trial. Sometimes these settlements are the consequence of negotiations that began long before the pretrial conference but simply culminated there. Sometimes the judge mediates the dispute and suggests a settlement agreeable to both sides.

If the disputants, however, insist on a trial, they can have one. In some instances they may obtain a jury trial, but as with criminal cases, most trials are held before a judge alone because litigants do not trust the lay judgment of jurors. Moreover, they may not want to incur the expense of a jury, which they must pay if they lose. The formal rules of evidence are supposed to govern the trial. The trial is usually a very formal ritual with testimony from witnesses, cross-examination by the other attorney, and finally a decision by the judge.

With few exceptions litigation can only be pursued with the help of attorneys. Plaintiffs (the complainants) and defendants can represent themselves, but such lay litigants operate under severe handicaps. They do not know the rules. They do not know how to choose among courts when several alternatives are available. They do not know the personnel as peers. They do not know the technical rules on which their case may falter. Hence, attorneys are almost indispensible when one is going to court.

The practical need to have an attorney means that civil courts have become much more the forum of the affluent than the poor. Indeed, in many cities courts have become instruments for controlling the poor and are used by powerful economic interests. This is particularly evident in two kinds of disputes: conflicts over indebtedness and those over rental agreements.

Most Americans live in debt; few purchase any of their major household items with cash. For low-income people, debt imposes an especially hard burden because they have no cushion for emergencies. When they are temporarily out of work or need extra money to meet medical expenses, their regular payments for their car, furniture, television set, and clothing lapse. Soon there develops a confrontation with the creditors, who often are not the stores where they purchased the goods but a finance company that took the loans over from the original merchant. Because the seller is no longer involved, consumers also have no effective recourse if the goods turn out to be faulty. The credit company is not interested, and the seller already has his money.[7]

When consumers fall behind in their payments, their accounts are often turned over to collection agencies, which make vigorous efforts to collect, including all kinds of harassment in addition to legal action. Collection agencies contact debtors and their employers, seeking all means legal (and sometimes illegal) to obtain payment. When they go to court, they seek to prove the legality of the debt and to obtain the use of court services to collect it. That may include obtaining permission to repossess the item purchased with the loan or to win payment by seizing other property from the debtor or seizing his or her wages (a process called wage garnishment).

As with all suits the creditor or collection agency files a complaint, which is then forwarded to the defendant. When defendants are poor, however, they often do not understand the notice that comes from the court. Indeed, in many cases the notice is not even given to defendants because the person who is supposed to serve the notice dumped it into the sewer rather than venture into the slum neighborhood where the defendant lives. Even when it is delivered, many defendants do not know what to do about it. Consider for instance the New York notice displayed in figure 8.1. This notice is written entirely in legalese. It does not tell the defendant how to respond, nor does it convey clearly what might happen if he or she does nothing. Rather, it threatens "judgment . . . against you for the relief demanded in the complaint," which is "annexed hereto." It does not say that something will be repossessed or seized or that wages will be held up.

The consequence is that most debtors do not respond to these summonses. Of course, many have no legal defense; the only reason

fig. 8.1
Summons Used in New York City Debt Collection Cases

YOU ARE HEREBY SUMMONED to appear in the Civil Court of the City of New York, County of New York, at the office of the Clerk of the said court at 111 Centre Street in the County of New York, City and State of New York, within the time period provided by law as noted below to make answer to the complaint which is annexed hereto; upon your failure to answer, judgment will be taken against you for the relief demanded in the complaint, together with the costs of this action.

Dated, New York, N.Y. _____ 196___

Plaintiff's Address   [Name and Address of
                                                           Plaintiff's Attorney]

Note: The law provides that:
   (a) If this summons is served by its delivery to you personally within the City of New York, you must appear and answer within TEN days after such service; *or*
   (b) If this summons is served by delivery to any person other than you personally, or is served outside the City of New York, *or by publication, or by any means other than personal delivery to you within the City of New York,* you are allowed THIRTY days after the proof of service thereof is filed with the Clerk of this Court within which to appear and answer.

Source: David Caplovitz, *Consumers in Trouble: A Study of Debtors in Default* (New York: The Free Press, 1974), p. 209.

they are not paying their debt is that they lack the money. But even those who might have a defense usually do not go to court to defend themselves. Ninety percent of these suits end as default judgments in Chicago, Detroit, and New York and probably in other cities as well.[8] The creditor or collection agency is authorized to proceed to the next step of seizing the debtor's property. If the debtor is working, that means contacting the employer. Often it also means that the debtor will soon lose his or her job. Employers do not like the extra work involved in processing wage garnishments, nor do employers like to have workers who appear to be irresponsible in their personal finances.

Even when debtors go to court, they are likely to find it an inhospitable place. If they do not have an attorney, no one is there to help them fill out the proper forms or to advise them about the required procedures. Further, the complainant, seeing that the defendant is present, may find an excuse to ask for a delay in the hearings to another day when the defendant is absent and a default judgment can be obtained. In any event, the defendants find that going to court is costly in time and aggravation. It is even more costly if an attorney is retained. Indeed, most cases of this sort do not warrant the expense of an attorney, and the defendants do not use one unless the lawyer comes from a free legal-assistance program.

That cost keeps many defendants from using lawyers in small-claims cases is particularly ironic because legal representation often brings more favorable outcomes in these disputes.[9] Having an attorney forces the other side to be more explicit in presenting evidence; it induces the judge to listen. It enables a defendant to use the informal norms of the courtroom. In many circumstances, however, the attorney costs more than the defendant can save by winning the lawsuit. That is one reason why so many defendants appear in small-claims court without lawyers. Complainants, on the other hand, often appear with lawyers. The law requires representation by an attorney if the complainant is a corporation; no one except a lawyer may represent it. But more significantly, complainants often process many cases before the court at the same time. Economies of scale permit them to retain attorneys.

Consequently, the courts where consumer debts are pursued— usually a city's small-claims courts—have become instruments of debt collection. They are regularly used by creditors and collection agencies to assist them in collecting delinquent debts. They rarely protect debtors against creditor abuses. They are more an extension of the commercial community than a neutral forum for the impartial adjudication of disputes.

The same appears to be true of some courts that process landlord complaints against tenants who have fallen behind in their rental payments. Chicago is a clear and perhaps extreme example.[10] In Chicago half of all tenants facing eviction do not file an appearance and many of those who file ultimately do not appear in court. When the tenant fails to appear, the landlord wins by default; even when the tenant appears, landlords win about 80 percent of their cases. This means they win not only the right to evict their tenant—if necessary, with the aid of the sheriff—but it also often means that they win a money judgment for back rents. Even more than consumer credit cases, eviction cases involve large numbers of people and a vital part of their lives. In Chicago during 1977, more than 64,000 eviction suits were filed, accounting for about one-quarter of all suits filed in the city's civil courts. If we assume that each suit involved a family of four, 250,000 persons faced eviction as a result of these suits. They also involved almost 10 percent of all rental units in the city of Chicago, but because these cases were concentrated in poorer areas, their impact is much greater in the ghettos and slums of the city than in middle-class areas. Yet only two judges heard all these cases at a pace of about one contested case every two minutes! Uncontested cases were heard at the rate of one every ten seconds.[11]

The reasons why tenants fare so poorly in Chicago's eviction court are much like those governing the failure of poor debtors in small-claims courts. The notices they receive are incomprehensible to many. This is particularly true for those persons who are literate only in Spanish; the documents are entirely in English. But even a good English-speaker would have difficulty with the notice shown in figure 8.2. In addition, lawyers for landlords often seek and obtain continuances when a tenant chances to appear on the right day for the trial. And even if the tenant testifies, the housing court judges often refuse to take the testimony seriously, although it is unrebutted. The judges simply fail to follow Illinois law requiring landlords to keep their property free from housing code violations in order to obtain full payment of their rents.

Both consumer credit suits and eviction cases typify a more general phenomenon: the unequal status of parties in civil-court suits when one of the parties has considerable resources and the other almost none. In such cases the courts become an extension of the more powerful party—an arm of the credit industry and landlord

fig. 8.2
Summons to Eviction Court in Chicago

Returnable in
ROOM NO. 602, CHICAGO CIVIC CENTER
9:30 A.M. Sharp
In the Circuit Court of Cook County, Illinois
Municipal Department, First District

Name All Parties

plaintiff—

No. _____

Amount claimed $ _____

defendant—

SUMMONS

To each defendant:

YOU ARE SUMMONED and required either:

1. To appear in person in Room 602, Chicago Civic Center, Chicago, Illinois, at 9:30 A.M. on _____, 19_____, OR

2. To file your written appearance by yourself or attorney in Room 602 at or before 9:30 A.M. on that date, OR

3. To file your answer to the complaint in Room 602 at or before 9:30 A.M. on that date. IF YOU FAIL TO DO SO, A JUDGMENT BY DEFAULT MAY BE TAKEN AGAINST YOU FOR THE RELIEF ASKED IN THE COMPLAINT, A COPY OF WHICH IS HERETO ATTACHED.

To the officer:

This summons must be returned by the officer or other person to whom it was given for service, with indorsement of service and fees, if any, immediately after service, and not less than 3 days before the day for appearance. If service cannot be made, this summons shall be returned so indorsed.

This summons may not be served later than 3 days before the day of appearance.

WITNESS _____, 19_____

_____
Clerk of court

Name
Attorney for
Address
City
Telephone

Date of service: _____, 19_____
[To be inserted by officer on copy left with
defendant or other person]

NOTICE TO PLAINTIFF

Not less than 28 or more than 40 days after issuance of summons if amount claimed is $1000 or less; not less than 21 or more than 40 days after issuance of summons if amount claimed is in excess of $1000.

NOTICE TO DEFENDANT

1. This case will not be heard on the day for appearance specified above. If you have filed your written appearance or answer, you need not appear in person on that day.

2. If the complaint is notarized, your answer must be notarized.

3. On the day for appearance specified above, the following will occur:
   a. If you have not obeyed this summons, a judgment or an order of default will be entered against you. Judgment is entered only if the amount claimed is liquidated, the complaint is notarized, and a military affidavit is filed. Otherwise proof will be taken in Room 1307 and judgment may be entered.
   b. If you are sued in forcible detainer, you need not file an answer. Your case will be heard on the 7th day after the day for appearance specified above, at 9:30 A.M. in a courtroom designated by the Presiding Judge.
   c. If you are sued for $1000 or less and no jury is demanded, you need not file an answer. Your case will be assigned for trial on the 14th day after the day for appearance specified above, at 9:30 A.M. in a courtroom designated by the Presiding Judge.
   d. In all other cases, if you have filed your appearance on time, you must file your answer not later than 10 days after the day for appearance specified above. On the day for appearance your case will be postponed 21 days to the Default-for-Want-of-Answer Call at 11:00 A.M. in Room 1307. On the Default-for-Want-of-Answer Call, if you have not filed your answer, a judgment or an order of default will be entered against you. But, if you have filed your answer, your case will be postponed for trial on a date in a courtroom designated by the Presiding Judge.

4. Late filing of an appearance or answer will not relieve you from a judgment or default order except by court order.

MORGAN M. FINLEY, CLERK OF THE CIRCUIT COURT OF COOK COUNTY

Source: Seymour J. Mansfield, ed., *Judgment Landlord: A Study of Eviction Court in Chicago* (Chicago, Ill.: Chicago Council of Lawyers, 1978), p. A28.

interests—rather than a neutral arbiter of disputes. The advantage accrues to the more powerful for several reasons. The more powerful parties in such disputes are "repeat players."[12] They use the courts again and again to obtain judgments. They gain experience with the procedures and develop ongoing relationships with court personnel. The court staff often tries to accommodate regular users because that helps the court regulate its input flow. For instance, in several Wisconsin cities it was not unusual for the court clerk to schedule all cases involving one particular creditor on the same day as a convenience to the creditor.[13] The creditor returned the favor by assuring the court that he would abide by customary procedures and not make life difficult for it. Thus, on the one side of these disputes are regular court users who become known to court personnel and who are to some degree trusted by them; on the other side are occasional defendants who usually are only names rather than people. When they do become real people, they generally do not know what to do and therefore are perceived as bothersome to court personnel and disruptive of the fast pace these courts are accustomed to.

In addition, repeat players usually engage attorneys who specialize in these particular proceedings. That concentrates the courts' business even more because a handful of attorneys handle many of a city's collection cases for hospitals, retail stores, and large landlords. In addition these attorneys develop an expertise in procedure that cannot be matched easily by defendants in these suits.

Repeat players also have the resources to play the odds in these cases. They do not need to win every case or win their case on the particular day it is scheduled. They have many cases and can afford to delay some and lose a few. They know from experience that 90 percent of their cases will go their way. Occasional users, however, cannot afford to wait or lose. The case is their only one. If they lose, they lose their apartment or their car, and their lives will be seriously disrupted. Although the stakes appear to be higher for them, they do not have sufficient resources to throw into the fight to assure victory. To the contrary, the outcome appears so surely unfavorable that occasional users often fail even to put up a fight.

Other disputes between private parties, such as personal-injury suits and divorces, are handled in a much more evenhanded manner by the courts. Personal-injury suits might appear at first glance to be in the same category as consumer credit and eviction cases since they involve occasional users as plaintiffs and insurance companies, who are repeat players, as defendants. This is not how it works out, however, because those who are injured and go to court do so with the service of an attorney who is also likely to be a repeat player. Representation by an attorney in personal-injury suits makes it much more likely that the insurance company will settle the case out of court.[14] If the case goes to court, the likelihood of success depends on having an attorney who is a repeat player, a specialist in these kinds of cases.[15] Since that often happens, courts that handle personal-injury cases have not become extensions of the insurance companies but play the more traditional role of the neutral adjudicator. A telltale sign of this is the fact that personal-injury cases are handled by the formal ritual of a bench or jury trial rather than through the abbreviated minute-and-a-half proceedings typifying consumer credit and eviction cases.

Divorce cases also involve equal opponents and almost always attorneys on at least one side. Many of the attorneys specialize to some degree in divorce proceedings and are repeat players in their courts.[16] Most of the cases are uncontested and only involve preparing the proper papers through prelitigation negotiations. The few contested cases generally involve attorneys who are equally familiar with divorce court procedures; like personal-injury trials, divorce trials tend to follow the formal, ritualistic pattern of the adversary process.

Cases involving businesses follow the same pattern. Most are marked by intensive negotiation before trial, and they go to trial only when negotiations fail. The litigants are rarely regular users of the courts, although the attorneys who represent business clients are often the litigation specialists of prominent firms and are repeat players. Generally, both sides to a business dispute are represented by such repeat players. Consequently, no one has a consistent advantage in court; the courts have not developed a reputation of favoring one side or another.

Cases involving disputes with city governments have quite varying characteristics. Some involve private individuals who seek exceptions to established policy; no grand political disputes are concerned. Others involve big firms who wish to develop large tracts of land; the consequences for other public services may be considerable.[17] Still other disputes concern policy issues such as busing children in the schools, equal employment opportunities for minorities in police and fire departments, or taxation policies. In such cases interest groups are likely to stand behind individual litigants.[18]

These cases almost always reflect the failure of negotiations. In most a long history of bargaining precedes the court battle. Both private parties and city officials seek to avoid confrontations, which are costly in both money and political standing. Most of these disputes also have to wend their way through administrative channels where prior efforts are made to settle them amicably. But some cannot be settled because the stakes are too high or because one side or the other finds itself incapable of accepting a proposed settlement. In such instances the disputants go to court.

Courts generally handle these kinds of cases in the most formal manner. Both sides typically have the resources to prepare their cases carefully. Both sides generally consider the possibility of an appeal from the outset, so they build the record of their case fully. Full-length trials typify these cases.

The adjudicatory process provides a political alternative to individuals and groups who are closed out of the legislative process because they are outsiders or because they lack other resources. Litigation becomes an alternative to politicking, and its consequences may be as significant. For instance, many school systems have been turned upside down by court busing orders. Alternatively, city plans to build freeways or other public facilities may be stalled for years in court litigation until they become too expensive to execute. This strategy is employed by some opponents of city policies who lack the power to block the project through city council action but who have sufficient resources to win delay through the courts.

Politics plays a rather muted role in the adjudication of civil conflicts. Political considerations are most evident in decisions by city agencies to go to court to defend a policy or to administer it. Such decisions are often a response to groups influential in city hall. For instance, even when school boards knew that they would lose litigation over school integration, they often went to court in response to white neighborhood interests who sought at least to win delay. Moreover, some especially sensitive political issues when brought to court are sometimes steered to sympathetic judges. That is most apparent in a city like Chicago where cases with strong political implications have traditionally gone to politically reliable judges. Such instances, however, are exceptional. Normally, politics rarely plays a direct, central role in adjudication, even when public agencies are the litigants.

City government's role in the adjudication of private and business disputes is even more marginal and political considerations are less significant. City budgetary decisions may be important in determining the level of support for legal assistance programs that help equalize the position of the poor in courtrooms. Housing policies play a significant role in determining the outcome of eviction suits, especially where the city's housing authority is the landlord seeking to evict tenants. But for most disputes, city politics is simply the background against which private conflicts are resolved.

impact of dispute processing

The existence of different types of dispute-processing institutions and their peculiar forms have differential effects on urban residents. The poor are the least well served; in many instances they are exploited by the existing dispute-processing institutions. Middle-class residents are perhaps the least affected. The city's commercial community is best served.

The poor are most explicitly exploited by the way in which adjudication impinges on them and constrains their other options. As we have seen, it is not uncommon for small-claims courts to become agents of debt collectors. Rather than protect the poor from unfair exploitation by creditors, many small-claims courts have become the tool of the creditor. When small-claims courts fail to provide the debtor with needed counsel or force an unwarranted settlement on the debtor when little justification exists for any additional payment, the small-claims court becomes part of the process through which creditors are encouraged to extend loans in dubious circumstances without being forced to accept the requisite risks. Creditors in many cities know that when a debtor defaults, the court stands ready to help them collect. Creditors in some cities know that even when damaged goods have been sold or promises to service appliances have not been kept, the court remains available to collect the debt.

An extreme case of bias against the poor exists in Chicago's eviction court. That court clearly has become an agent of landlords. Only when tenants appear with counsel do they stand a chance of even being heard. When they come to court alone, they are often not allowed to present their case. If—in the unusual circumstance—they are given their two minutes, nothing they say makes any difference. Judgment for the landlord is a foregone conclusion. We do not know how common such abuses are in other cities. There is every reason to suspect that they exist in some, because the conditions in Chicago's eviction court simply take to the extreme the circumstances that lead to unfair treatment of the poor: the pairing off of repeat players against one-shotters, with repeat players gaining their advantage through their greater resources, greater expertise, better contacts, and ability to play for long-term results rather than immediate victory.

Thus, in two important arenas of conflict, the poor are effectively shut out of the adjudicatory process. They can rarely win; they generally lose. The result is that when they are forced to negotiate with creditors or landlords, they do so at a severe disadvantage. Creditors and landlords can threaten to go to court and win everything; debtors and tenants have no credible threat. Mediation is also not usually a viable alternative because debtors and tenants rarely share the common cultural and social bonds with their adversaries that might make mediation a success. Creditors and landlords are often impersonal corporations that cannot be shamed into compromise. That leaves the poor only one alternative: avoidance. Large numbers use avoidance to escape conflicts arising from indebtedness and late rentals. But even escape is not always possible since debt collectors increasingly rely on computer searches of Social Security numbers to locate debtors who have fled to new neighborhoods or other cities. Likewise, it is often difficult for the poor to find alternative housing, especially when a large part of the low-income housing market in a city is controlled by a single landlord—the public-housing authority. Thus, the justice system of most cities is effectively closed to their poor residents for some important cases. They have few ways of resisting disputes with more powerful adversaries.

The situation is quite different for middle-class residents. They are not heavy users of the civil courts, nor are they as likely to be abused by them. Conflicts over credit and housing occur less frequently because middle-class people do not fall behind in their payments as readily as the poor and because they are more likely to own rather than rent their residences. But even when faced with the same problems as the poor, they confront their adversary from a much more advantageous position. They are more likely to find an attorney whom they can afford to retain, and with legal assistance they can equalize the contest considerably. Because they stand a chance in court, they are much more likely to fare well in out-of-court negotiations. It is even more likely that some mediation succeeds in their conflicts because the cultural gap between the corporate creditor or landlord and themselves is much less than with the poor. Finally, they can indulge in avoidance or escape more readily. They can better afford simply to lump it and accept the loss than can the poor; they also have more alternative sources of housing if they decide to move.

The adjudicatory process in civil disputes is most of all a service to a city's commercial community. City businesses make the most extensive use of the courts and have in some instances succeeded in making the courts an instrument of their own profit-seeking ventures. That is most apparent in credit and housing operations, but it may also be true for other elements of a city's commercial life where adjudication is an important part of the business routine. Many businesses, of course, avoid litigation and prefer to negotiate. This occurs most often when the adversary is someone whose continued beneficence is required—for instance, a supplier or important commercial customer. Even those businesses that do not rely on litigation find the courts open to them, however; they generally stand a fifty-fifty chance of winning if they go to court.

Commercial enterprises also find alternative dispute processing-mechanisms available. Negotiations proceed from the certain knowledge that adjudication is a viable next step should the negotiations fail. Mediation is also frequently used because commercial enterprises operate in a common cultural milieu with many of their adversaries. They often belong to the same trade association, which offers a mediation service; they frequently share membership in the city's chamber of commerce, which may also offer mediation. Thus, it seems likely that commercial firms need to resort to avoidance much less frequently than individual disputants and certainly less often than the poor.

Unequal access to civil justice is not inevitable. Indeed, it does not prevail in other kinds of disputes: the personal-injury suit and the divorce case. The reason is a combination of circumstances and explicit public policy. In divorce disputes, both adversaries are likely to be equally powerless. Public policy has promoted prelitigation negotiations, reserving the true adjudicatory process for the remaining contested cases. In personal-injury disputes, public policy has replaced adjudication with negotiation where no-fault statutes exist. In these states the injured party files a claim, and if it is disputed, the law provides mechanisms for negotiation and administrative arbitration. Where the fault principle still governs, injured persons can often find an attorney because lawyers are willing to take cases on a contingent-fee basis as long as there is a reasonable chance of recovering a claim. The lawyers who tend to get most of these cases are somewhat specialized and can negotiate with insurance companies with some success. It is also in the insurance company's interest to make a point of paying out benefits as well as collecting premiums. Consequently, the class differential in processing personal-injury claims is much less severe than in creditor or eviction cases.

If they wished, cities could do much more to equalize access to their adjudicatory forums. Most cities spend very little of their own money to provide legal services for the poor, and they spend little on alternative structures to courts for providing mediation and arbitration services. Few cities use their links to judges to pressure the courts to change procedures so that they are more readily open to the poor.

Such changes might involve merely altering the legal forms sent out as summonses so that ordinary people can comprehend them. It might mean providing more court time for certain categories of cases—in Chicago, for example, extending the court call for eviction cases from one and a half to five hours a day.

Civil justice, however, has not enjoyed the political limelight of criminal proceedings. The concerns in the civil-justice field are too clearly based on class and ethnic groups. Denying poor blacks access to the courts does not threaten the middle-class constituencies of the political leaders in American cities in the same way that a crime wave in the ghetto does. Consequently, there is much less impetus for reform.

--- **notes** ---

1 William L. F. Felstiner, "Influences of Social Organization on Dispute Processing," *Law and Society Review*, 9, (1974), 79–80, provides a general discussion of avoidance.

2 P. H. Gulliver, "Negotiations as a Mode of Dispute Settlement: Towards a General Model," *Law and Society Review*, 7 (1973), 667–91.

3 H. Laurence Ross, *Settled out of Court* (Chicago, Ill.: Aldine, 1970).

4 Richard Danzig and Michael J. Lowy, "Everyday Disputes and Mediation in the United States: A Reply to Professor Felstiner," *Law and Society Review*, 9 (1975), 682–91; Daniel McGillis and Joan Mullen, *Neighborhood Justice Centers* (Washington, D.C.: U.S. Department of Justice, Law Enforcement Assistance Administration, 1975).

5 John A. Hannigan, "Newspaper Ombudsman and Consumer Complaints: An Empirical Assessment," *Law and Society Review*, 11 (1977), 679–99.

6 John Paul Ryan and others, *America's Trial Judges at Work: The Role of Organizational Influences* (New York: The Free Press, 1979), ch. 3.

7 The credit company may be held legally liable for claims made by the seller, but in practice such liability is difficult to enforce.

8 David Caplovitz, *Consumers in Trouble: A Study of Debtors in Default* (New York: The Free Press, 1974), p. 221.

9 Barbara Yngvesson and Patricia Hennessey, "Small Claims, Complex Disputes: A Review of the Small Claims Literature," *Law and Society Review*, 9, (1975), 250–51; Austin Sarat, "Alternatives in Dispute Processing: Litigation in a Small Claims Court," *Law and Society Review*, 10 (1976), 366–68.

10 Seymour J. Mansfield, ed., *Judgment Landlord: A Study of Eviction Court in Chicago* (Chicago, Ill.: Chicago Council of Lawyers, 1978).

11 Ibid., especially pp. 33–100.

12 Marc Galanter, "Why the Haves Come out Ahead: Speculation on the Limits of Legal Change," *Law and Society Review*, 9 (1974), 95–160.

13 Herbert Jacob, *Debtors in Court* (Chicago, Ill.: Rand McNally, 1969), pp. 99–100.

14 Ross, *Settled Out of Court*, pp. 193–98.

15 Douglas E. Rosenthal, *Lawyer and Client: Who's in Charge* (New York: Russell Sage Foundation, 1974), pp. 99–102.

16 Galanter, focusing on the litigants in divorce cases rather than on their attorneys, classifies them as involving one-shotters; see "Why the Haves Come out Ahead," p. 107.

17 See Kenneth M. Dolbeare, *Trial Courts in Urban Politics* (New York: John Wiley & Sons, 1967).

18 Dolbeare asserts that interest groups play only a small role in public civil litigation, but he did not examine civil rights litigation; ibid., pp. 39–40.

variations in concluding civil conflicts: a closer look at four wisconsin cities

$t$he great variety of civil disputes and the circumstances under which they are concluded give a distinctive cast to civil justice in each city. The common elements we discussed in the preceding two chapters allow us to identify some of the most important dimensions of civil justice in American cities. But as with criminal justice, it is useful to look at a handful of cities in detail to see how justice varies from one city to another.* The disputes we shall examine involve private citizens and business firms in conflicts over unpaid bills. Business firms actively seek to collect their debts. To maximize their collections, they may negotiate but often they resort to adjudication. Debtors, by contrast, often seek to avoid conflict; they may do so by fleeing or by obtaining a bankruptcy judgment, which nullifies their indebtedness.

The cities we shall examine are Green Bay, Racine, Kenosha, and Madison. In the mid-1960s, when the study was conducted, Green Bay was the smallest of the four; it is largely a trading center with some manufacturing. Known for its professional football team, the Packers, Green Bay is by far the smallest city to have a National Football League team. Racine and Kenosha are manufacturing centers located just

---

* This chapter is adapted from Herbert Jacob, "Wage Garnishment and Bankruptcy Proceedings in Four Wisconsin Cities," in *City Politics and Public Policy*, ed. James Q. Wilson. Copyright © 1968 John Wiley & Sons, Inc. Reprinted by permission of John Wiley & Sons, Inc.

south of Milwaukee and north of Chicago. They are independent cities but part of the large metropolitan complex that stretches from the steel mills of northern Indiana through Chicago to Milwaukee. Madison is the capital of Wisconsin and the site of the University of Wisconsin. It is more a white-collar town than the other cities, but it does have some manufacturing.

At the time of the study, Green Bay was the most traditional of the four cities in terms of its institutional structures, its economy, and its governmental processes. It was least affected by professionalism and bureaucracy; it had retained many personalized ways of doing business. Madison, at the other extreme, was the most modernized city. Both business and government handled their affairs bureaucratically with standardized, impersonal norms governing relationships between seller and buyer or agency and client.

Two forms of legal action were particularly prominent in the conflict over unsettled debts: wage garnishments and personal bankruptcies. Both occurred commonly in the mid-1960s. More than 100,000 persons petitioned federal courts for bankruptcy status, and each year at least ten times as many wage garnishments were filed in the United States.[1] The widespread use of these courts was partially due to the economic circumstances governing consumer purchases after World War II.

The amount of consumer credit has grown rapidly during the twentieth century. Americans can no longer be characterized as a people bent on saving; it is much more accurate to describe them as a people bent on spending. In the forty-five years following 1920, consumer credit grew from $40 per capita to $72 per capita in standardized dollars.[2]

As Katona points out, credit was used to purchase large items that were unavailable to previous generations of consumers.[3] In many cases credit purchases enabled peopled to buy machines instead of making the daily or weekly transactions formerly required to buy services similar to those rendered by the machines. Thus, television provided many families with a substitute for movies and other entertainment; the washer and dryer supplanted the neighborhood laundry; the vacuum cleaner replaced the maid; the home freezer liberated the housewife from daily trips to the corner grocery and allowed her to shop once a week at the supermarket no matter how large her family. According to the "1967 Survey of Consumer Finances," almost half of the population had installment debts for such items. Half of those who were indebted had obligations over $1,000; more than half had to commit more than 10 percent of their income to debt repayment.[4]

The rise of consumer indebtedness was largely the product of economic and social developments after World War II.[5] The increasingly widespread ownership of cars and the growth of suburbia played a central role in the expansion of consumer credit in the United States.

At the end of World War II savings were high, and the desire to purchase large consumer goods that the depression and war had placed out of reach was even higher. Two already traditional items were on the shopping lists of many Americans—a new car and a home of their own. The purchase of new cars increased rapidly after the war, and the new cars cost a great deal more than the prewar models. The demand for housing was equally pressing. New housing developments sprang up overnight. The desire for home ownership together with the availability of automobiles promoted the rapid development of suburban communities.

The purchase of both new cars and new houses was financed largely on credit. Automobile manufacturers had experimented since the 1920s with credit sales and had managed to expand their market by making credit purchasing relatively easy and respectable. Homes, because they involve far larger sums of money, had long been financed on credit. After 1945, however, the GI Bill of Rights made home loans more readily available to the large number of veterans just released from the armed forces. Borrowing to purchase a home also became more widespread.

The purchase of a home led to other consumer capital expenditures. Homes need furnishings. Stoves and refrigerators were already standard equipment in the kitchen; soon to be added were washers, dryers, dishwashers, air conditioners, and television sets.

The growth of credit purchasing extended, however, beyond the acquisition of capital goods. With the widespread use of installment purchases, Americans also become more accustomed to buying consumable goods on credit. Gasoline and oil for their cars were increasingly purchased on "thirty day" accounts with credit cards; department stores began offering "revolving" accounts, which enabled consumers to purchase as much as several hundred dollars worth of clothing, housewares, or other small items and pay for them over an eighteen-month or two-year period.[6] Under these arrangements, the consumer was in constant debt to the store. Payments fluctuated only slightly with the size of the debt; the upper limit of purchases was relatively high. Indebtedness to other sources also increased. The habit of paying one's doctor on the spot decreased; instead, people expected a bill at the end of the month. Only in food purchases did credit usage shrink as the corner grocery with its informal credit system was replaced by the cash-and-carry supermarket.

The procurement of loans from small loan companies also increased. In some cases these companies extended loans to cover the purchase of particular items and served as an alternative to the bank or the store for installment purchases. In other cases, however, personal loans were made for miscellaneous purposes—to consolidate bills, to purchase a number of smaller items, to buy Christmas presents, or to pay a pressing bill.

A final dimension of the rise of consumer credit was the dependence of merchants for profit on credit as compared to profit on the sale of merchandise.[7] Competition on the price of goods was far greater than on the price of credit.[8] Except for home mortgages and automobile loans, few consumers shopped for credit. Consequently, many merchants found that credit transactions were particularly profitable, and there was a very heavy emphasis in advertising and among some sales personnel toward credit purchases. Until specifically outlawed by the Truth in Lending Act of 1968, some advertisements did not even mention cash prices but informed potential consumers only of the down payment and the size of monthly payments for an unspecified period of time.

The increased use of credit was supported by a very large rise in the income of the average American. The median family income almost doubled from $3,894 in 1947 to $6,262 in 1965 in standardized dollars.[9] Moreover, better job security, more widespread health insurance, and broader coverage through private and public old-age pension plans made larger parts of a person's net income available for immediate consumption. People felt safer in committing their income to the repayment of loans as they no longer felt so pressing a need to save for a rainy day. Hence, more people were able to afford credit and could purchase a wider range of goods.

By the mid-1960s, almost three-fourths of all young families with a child under six had some installment debt, and only 11 percent of the whole population asserted that they never used installment credit.[10] As figure 9.1 shows, in 1967 only the very poor, the very rich, and the very old were infrequent debtors. The very poor were unable to obtain credit; the very rich did not need it. The very old were also often quite poor; in addition, they had less need for many of the capital purchases that younger Americans made. Moreover, it is likely that the older consumers were more conservative, having grown up in an era when indebtedness was less socially acceptable.

Data from Wisconsin show that the characteristics of credit users

fig. 9.1
The Relationship of Income and Age with Indebtedness in Wisconsin and the United States

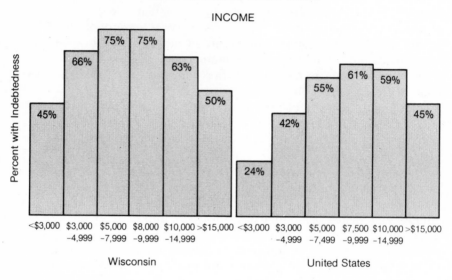

INCOME

Wisconsin

United States

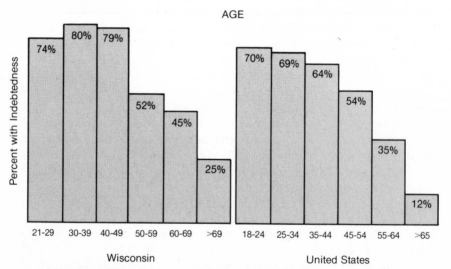

AGE

Wisconsin

United States

Source for United States data: "1967 Survey of Consumer Finances," mimeographed, Statistical Report VIII (Ann Arbor: University of Michigan Survey Research Center), table VIII–3.

Source for Wisconsin data: 1965 Wisconsin Survey (Madison: University of Wisconsin Survey Research Laboratory).

described by Katona and the Michigan Survey Research Center for the nation were consistent with those in Wisconsin in 1965, although the level of installment indebtedness in Wisconsin was about 10 percent higher than in the nation as a whole. Installment buying was much more common among Wisconsinites between twenty-one and fifty years of age than among those over fifty. The group most likely to use installment credit was those between twenty-one and fifty-four, with no children yet in college but an expectation of sending some there, and with an income under $9,000. Of this group, 86 percent were credit users. An even higher proportion of credit users were those people in low-paying white- and blue-collar occupations with incomes between $5,000 and $9,000; 97 percent of this group used credit.[11]

Thus, the potential for conflict over credit use was very widespread in Wisconsin in the mid-1960s. It was not concentrated among the poor. To the contrary, the greatest potential for conflict existed among the lower middle class.

When debtors fail to meet their obligations, creditors have a number of potential remedies. The particular remedies that can be used depend in large part on the kind of security obtained when the loan is made.[12] If the loan is made on a security guaranteed by a chattel mortgage, the creditor can move to foreclose on the mortgage and have the property that served as security sold. If the loan is made through a conditional sales contract, the title of the property (e.g., a washing machine) remains in the hands of the lender, who can repossess the item if the borrower has defaulted. If the loan is made without any security, as many consumer loans are, then the creditor has to go to court to seize some property of the debtor—car (if owned outright), house (subject to the same restriction), bank account, or wages.

Repossession on a conditional sales contract was the most expeditious creditor remedy in the 1960s. No court action was required. The creditor could repossess whenever the debtor fell behind on payments. If the debtor felt wronged, he or she could sue for damages, but the creditor had the initiative and could move at will. In reality, of course, both social and economic constraints deterred hasty repossession because the hasty repossesser could lose potential customers who heard of his or her actions. In addition, the item was often not worth as much as the debtor owed, so it was to the creditor's economic advantage to have the debtor repay in full—even if over a longer period of time—than to repossess merchandise that would bring only a fraction of the debt on the secondhand market. Thus, creditors often sought to negotiate with delinquent debtors rather than repossess.

The other remedies require court action. On a mortgage, the creditor has to move in court to foreclose and then use the services of the sheriff to seize the property, have it sold, and obtain the funds in partial or full payment of the debt. If a bank account or wages are to be seized and transferred, the lender has to prove the legitimacy of the debt by obtaining a favorable judgment in a court suit.

In actual practice these proceedings, although time consuming and expensive, occurred with almost mechanical regularity. Some lenders extended credit merely on the signature of a note that confessed judgment—meaning that the creditor only needed to file the note with the appropriate court to prove the validity of the debt. The debtor had no opportunity to dispute the legitimacy of the claim.[13] Then to collect the debt, creditors sought to seize some property belonging to the debtor.

The seizure of a debtor's bank account or wages is called garnishment. Its legal foundation lies in common-law usage, and it came to America as an English custom. Garnishment obliges a third party to give to the court whatever property of a debtor that party holds. Most garnishments are against wages. The debtor's bank or employer is ordered to pay out whatever it possesses of the debtor's. The bank or employer who refuses becomes liable for the debt. If the claim is legitimate, the court then turns the funds over to the creditor. Garnishment itself is not the issue of the court case but is a means of executing the court's decision in the judgment suit.[14]

In Wisconsin as in most other states, not all of a person's wages were subject to seizure; a portion was exempt. In Wisconsin there were two kinds of exemptions. One was a subsistence allowance automatically applied by the employer, who was ordered by the court to pay a certain amount of the paycheck to the debtor regardless of the garnishment. In the mid-1960s the subsistence allowance consisted of one-half of the garnishee's pay, or $25 if the debtor was single and $40 if he or she was married, whichever amount was smaller. The amount to be paid did not depend on the length of the pay period; it was the same $25 or $40 whether the pay period was a week or a month. A second kind of exemption—considerably more generous and more complicated to calculate—was available to debtors in Wisconsin if they went to court to contest the garnishment. But since most garnishees did not go to court, they obtained only the $25 or $40 the employer was told to disburse.[15] Consequently, most delinquent debtors in these Wisconsin cities were left with only a very small portion of their paycheck.

For Wisconsin creditors the garnishment process was not unduly complicated, although they needed to pay some attention to detail.[16] They had to go to court and fill out a summons. On the summons, they listed their complaint, the amount due, the name and address of the debtor, and the name and address of the debtor's employer. The summons had to be delivered to the employer on payday. No other day would do because the employer technically did not hold any property of the debtor except on the day the wages became due. Thus, the lender needed to know the correct name and address of the debtor's employer and the correct payday. With this knowledge and the payment of fees for filing and for the delivery of the summons (by mail or by a sheriff's deputy), the process was complete. If the creditor caught the employer on the correct day, most of the paycheck was sent to the court. Several days later (usually ten), there was a brief hearing on whether to turn the amount caught in the garnishment over to the creditor. At this stage the debtor could appear to defend himself or herself. If there had been a confession of judgment or a default judgment, however, the debtor usually did not have a substantial legal defense. Nevertheless, appearance at this time afforded the lender and the customer an opportunity to negotiate a private agreement that usually involved the promise to resume payment. The lender then retained part of the garnished wages as the first of these new payments and released the remainder to the debtor. In Wisconsin only one creditor could garnish a person's wages on a single payday, but every payday one or another of the debtor's creditors might be waiting to seize the paycheck.

Debtors also had some legal remedies to conclude disputes about their debts. The most frequent was to declare oneself bankrupt. The Constitution reserves to Congress the right to pass bankruptcy laws. Furthermore, the Constitution forbids the states to pass laws that impair contracts, but it imposes no such restriction on the federal government. Consequently, only federal laws can discharge a debtor of past debts and make them legally void. This is what bankruptcy does.

Two kinds of remedies are available for the ordinary consumer under bankruptcy legislation. The first is called a Wage-Earner's Plan, or Chapter 13 (from the section of the act); it may be described as bankruptcy on the installment plan.[17] It allows the debtor a reasonable time (usually not more than three years) to repay debts. All debts listed by the debtor are included. All secured creditors and a majority of unsecured creditors must agree to the plan. When sufficient agreement is secured, all creditors are included whether they themselves approved or not. The probability of agreement is heightened by a number of strategems in common use. Typically, for instance, the ballots mailed to creditors state that if they are not returned, agreement will be inferred from the creditor's silence. Failure to return a ballot is interpreted to mean assent, and court officials count such absent ballots as favorable votes. Moreover, it is often possible to convert recalcitrant secured creditors (who could veto the plan) to an unsecured status by forcing them to repossess their security; any balance then remaining is an unsecured debt. As unsecured creditors, such lenders can cast a negative vote but they have lost their veto.[18] A further advantage for the debtor is that the plan can provide for partial payment rather than full repayment. In that case, or if the debtor is unable to repay according to the plan, he or she can petition for a full discharge of the remaining debts under bankruptcy. Throughout the plan's duration the debtor is completely protected against any legal action or other harassment by creditors. The federal court issues an injunction that prohibits such proceedings; any violator of the injunction risks contempt of court proceedings.

Such Chapter 13 provisions also impose a considerable burden on the debtor. Debtors must agree to make regular (weekly, biweekly, or monthly) payments to a special officer of the court called a trustee who then forwards the money to the creditors. In many instances the debtor's entire paycheck is paid directly to the trustee, who gives the debtor a "living allowance" and retains the rest to pay creditors. The trustee's costs are also paid by the debtor. Under some circumstances, enrollment in a Chapter 13 plan may resemble peonage, for the debtor is under the firm supervision of the trustee. Enrollment, however, is entirely voluntary (supported sometimes by strong informal pressures, as for instance the urging of one's employer), and the debtor may withdraw from the plan at any time. Withdrawal is not punishable.

Bankruptcy is much simpler. Debtors list all their debts and all their assets. All that debtors need show is that their current debts exceed their current assets. Unless creditors can demonstrate that the debtor obtained their funds through fraud and unless the debtor has already been through bankruptcy in the previous six years, the debtor is entitled to a discharge of his or her debts. The federal court receiving the petition has no discretion to refuse a discharge except for fraud or ineligibility because of earlier use of bankruptcy.

The debtor's assets, such as they are, will be seized to repay the creditors as fully as possible. Most bankrupts, however, have no significant assets because state exemption statutes are often quite generous and have been incorporated in the federal bankruptcy law. So it was that all the properties listed in Wisconsin's exemption statutes were free from seizure in a bankruptcy proceeding. Debtors who owned cars worth $1,000 could keep them; if they had life insurance with a cash value of less than $5,000, they could keep it.[19] The same held true for the other articles named in the exemption statute. Prudent attorneys for bankrupts would have their clients convert as much of their assets as possible into an exempt form. Thus, bankrupts were not necessarily penniless after they left bankruptcy court; they left with all properties exempted by Wisconsin law. In actual practice, however, many bankrupts owned little of even this kind of property.

Bankrupts also did not leave bankruptcy court without any debts. Some debts may not be discharged through bankruptcy. Tax bills, whether from the federal, state, or local government, are not affected by bankruptcy. Nor can alimony or child-support payments be discharged in bankruptcy.[20] In addition, debtors can choose to reaffirm the discharged debts at any time after bankruptcy. Bankrupts who volunteer to repay some of the debts wiped out through bankruptcy are free to do so, and these obligations again become legally binding upon them. Many debtors reaffirm some of their debts in order to keep certain household goods; consequently, many debtors do not leave bankruptcy court completely free of their debts.

The legal system thus provided creditors and debtors a set of conflicting and intertwining remedies. Creditors could protect themselves by requiring adequate security. Competitive pressures, however, often induced them to extend credit without security and without adequate information to evaluate the risk they were taking. They could protect themselves even in these circumstances by selling on a conditional sales contract or with a confession of judgment, but neither helped if the merchandise depreciated quickly or if the creditor was selling services rather than goods. When all else failed, creditors could seize their debtors' wages through garnishment proceedings. On the debtors' side, bankruptcy provided a potentially effective remedy. They could protect much of their equity through bankruptcy and wipe out most of their debts. In practice, however, its effectiveness approached the theoretical optimum only when essential goods did not serve as security for some of the debts. When they did, debtors often reaffirmed the debt after bankruptcy to retain goods they needed and were accustomed to.

The legal framework channels creditor-debtor conflicts into a very few solutions. Creditors are provided opportunities to seize assets of their delinquent debtors. Because the credit system itself leaves most debtors with few assets other than wages, wages become a prime target for creditors. The legal system exacerbates this tendency by providing a convenient and relatively simple mechanism for seizing wages. Bankruptcy is the principal remedy used by debtors.

Residents of the four Wisconsin cities, however, used these remedies at quite different rates. As table 9.1 indicates, the incidence of garnishments varied from 2.1 per 1,000 people in Green Bay to 30.7 per 1,000 in Racine. The variation in bankruptcy was not quite so great; it ranged from 0.62 per 1,000 in Green Bay to 1.32 per 1,000 in Racine. Similar variations existed for general civil litigation in the four counties in which the four cities were located. As table 9.2 shows, civil litigation varied from 8.2 per 1,000 population in Brown County (Green Bay) to 27.0 per 1,000 in Racine.

One possible explanation for the differences in the use of court services in these four cities might be their socioeconomic characteristics. Table 9.3 displays the data on a variety of socioeconomic indicators for the four cities. They are arranged in the ascending order of their litigation rates, with Green Bay first (the lowest litigation rate) and Racine last (the highest litigation rate).

Table 9.3 shows that the cities varied somewhat in their socioeconomic characteristics. Madison was the largest, was the wealthiest (as measured by bank deposits per capita), and had the highest proportion of well-educated citizens. Green Bay, Kenosha, and Racine differed less between each other. Racine had the highest nonwhite population; Green Bay had the smallest proportion in manufacturing (it was a railway center). As the largest city of the relatively prosperous Fox River Valley and northeastern Wisconsin, Green Bay also had the highest per capita retail sales volume.

None of these differences, however, appears to be related to the

table 9.1
Garnishment and Bankruptcy Actions for Twelve-Month Period:
Gross Totals and Actions per Population by City

	madison	**racine**	**kenosha**	**green bay**
Garnishments	2860	2740	813	130
per 1000 population	22.6	30.7	12.0	2.1
Bankruptcies	112	100	63	32
Chapter 13 users	37	18	5	7
Total bankrupt-13's				
per 1000 population	1.17	1.32	1.0	.62

table 9.2
Civil Cases in Four Counties, July 1, 1964–July 1, 1965

	dane (madison)	racine	kenosha	brown (green bay)
County and Circuit Court	1691	817	1203	803
Small Claims Court (minus garnishment)	4203	3024	743	233
Civil cases per 1000 population	26.5	27.0	19.5	8.2

Source: Wisconsin Judicial Council, "1965 Judicial Statistics," mimeographed (Madison: Wisconsin Judicial Council), table 1.

varying litigation rates of the four cities. If socioeconomic background factors were determinative, one would expect the highest garnishment and bankruptcy rate in the city with the highest retail volume. To the contrary, the garnishment-bankruptcy rate was lowest in that city (Green Bay). One might expect garnishments and bankruptcies to be most frequent in the cities with the larger proportion of middle-income families, for it was among them that garnishment and bankruptcy occurred most often. Table 9.3 shows that the proportions of middle-income families were rather similar in the four cities, however; it was highest in Green Bay, the city with the lowest litigation rate, and second highest in Racine, the city with the highest litigation rate.

table 9.3
Selected Socioeconomic Indicators for the Four Cities

	green bay	kenosha	madison	racine
Population (1960)	62,888	67,889	126,706	89,144
Percentage nonwhite (1960)	.4	.5	1.9	5.4
Percentage with high school + education	46.3	36.8	65.3	40.6
Percentage with incomes between $3,000–$10,000 (1960)	76.1	69.1	68.9	71.6
Percentage of labor force in manufacturing (1960)	26.9	50.6	15.1	49.1
Number of manufacturing establishments with 20+ employees (1958)	42	37	45	82
Per capita retail sales (1958)	$1892	$1199	$1520	$1344
Per capita bank demand deposits (1960)	$742	$558	$931	$724

Source: Bureau of the Census, *City County Data Book, 1962,* pp. 566–74.

Table 9.4 presents more sophisticated socioeconomic measurements for the four cities. For each of them, its decile position vis-à-vis all other American cities of more than 25,000 population is given for five factors, each of which is the result of an analysis involving a large number of individual measurements.[21] Against this larger framework, it is also clear that the four Wisconsin cities did not differ among themselves in such a way that we may explain the wide variation in their civil-litigation rate. Consequently, we must conclude that socioeconomic characteristics are not related to variations in the litigation rate.

A study by Alford and Scoble of the same four Wisconsin cities suggests that they represent four distinct political cultures.[22] The authors define political culture in terms of leadership orientations, mass orientations, and public norms prevalent in the cities. The four types they distinguish are (1) *traditional conservatism* (Green Bay), where "government is seen as essentially passive, as a caretaker of law and order, not as an active instrument either for social goals or private goals"; (2) *traditional liberalism* (Kenosha), where "the bargaining process may even extend to traditional services"; (3) *modern conservatism* (Racine), where "government is seen as legitimately active, but furthering private economic interests which are regarded as in the long range public interest"; and (4) *modern liberalism* (Madison), where "a high level of political involvement . . . may itself exacerbate conflicts."

Alford and Scoble concentrated their analysis on the kinds of public decisions made in the four cities and the relationship between these cultural types and the manner in which choices were made over

table 9.4
Socioeconomic Profiles of the Four Wisconsin Cities

	green bay	kenosha	racine	madison
Median income	4	8	7	7
Deprivation Index	3	4	2	0
Percentage single dwelling units	3	2	2	1
Percentage nonwhite	2	3	5	3
Density	3	7	3	8

The figures in the table indicate the decile in which each city ranks when compared to all other American cities with 25,000 or more inhabitants in 1960.

Source: Jeffrey K. Hadden and Edgary F. Borgatta, *American Cities* (Chicago, Ill.: Rand McNally, 1965), pp. 99–100.

public controversies. The decision of private citizens to use a public service like the courts is a choice of quite a different order. It does not involve public controversy; the decision is made privately by individual citizens and firms rather than through the public decision-making agencies. Nevertheless, the decisions involve a choice for or against invoking public processes for private purposes. Such choices may be influenced by leadership and mass orientations toward public life as well as by public norms about what constitutes appropriate use of governmental facilities.

Juxtaposing the Alford-Scoble typology against tables 9.1 and 9.2 suggests that political culture may be a significant explanation for the differences in litigation rates. The two traditional cities have the lower litigation rates, while the two modern cities have the higher litigation rates. Whereas Alford and Scoble find that the liberalism-conservatism scale accounts for much of the difference in the style and content of public decision-making, the data on litigation suggest that the degree of traditionalism or modernity is the more relevant element of political culture affecting the propensity to use court services.

The traditional political culture, according to Alford and Scoble, is characterized by a relatively low level of bureaucratization in government and a hesitance to invoke governmental processes. In a modern political culture government is more bureaucratized. This means that relationships between agency and client are on a legalistic and impersonal footing, whereas in a traditional culture the citizen is likely to approach the official or be received by him or her as an acquaintance rather than as a stranger. In addition, there is greater reliance on private dispute-settling processes in a traditional culture than in a modern one. In the more traditional culture people make greater efforts to negotiate settlements between themselves as neighbors and friends. Because they feel they know one another on a personal basis, they have more opportunities to settle conflicts within the confines of established private relationships. Not so in the more modern city. Personal relationships are more strained; people deal with one another more on a business and impersonal basis than as friends and neighbors. Consequently, they feel less confidence in using private dispute-settling procedures. Conversely, people in the modern city are more willing to invoke the public processes of government for solving their problems, be they a neighborhood development program needing a city council decision or a creditor-debtor conflict that requires the services of a court.

The data on the use of wage garnishments and bankruptcies in the four Wisconsin cities provides some support for this interpretation. The process of taking a debtor to court in order to collect a loan is a highly impersonal proceeding involving the use of public officials as intermediaries (the sheriff serves the papers). As such, we would expect it to occur more frequently in the more modern cities. We might also expect public perceptions and norms to support the lesser use of the courts in Green Bay and Kenosha and the greater use of the courts in Racine and Madison. The evidence indicates that this in fact occurred. Interviews with attorneys showed that creditors in Green Bay and Kenosha were more reluctant to turn accounts over to lawyers than those in Racine and Madison. Moreover, when they did give delinquent accounts to a lawyer, these accounts were more likely to have been more thoroughly worked over than those in Racine and Madison. These comments by attorneys were supported by the results of a questionnaire sent to creditors in the four cities. In the traditional cities slightly more creditors made use of personal contacts, telephone calls to the debtor, and contacts with employers than in the modern ones. In addition, fewer creditors in Green Bay and Kenosha thought that eliminating garnishment would make a difference to their operations; this response apparently reflected their lesser reliance on court proceedings for collecting delinquent accounts. Finally, in Green Bay where the garnishment rate was lowest, both attorneys and creditors in personal interviews often asserted that the city was small enough for everyone to know everyone else and that this made court action unnecessary. In fact, Green Bay had only 5,000 fewer inhabitants than Kenosha, where no respondents mentioned the intimacy of the city, and was only one-third smaller than Racine with its high garnishment rate. The perception of Green Bay as a small town, however, fits our characterization of its culture as traditional and hostile to litigation.

The lower garnishment rate in the traditional cities also fits Alford and Scoble's description of these cities as ones in which the business elite does not look upon government as a legitimate instrument for obtaining private objectives. If the business managers who extended credit took their cue from the leaders of the business community, we would expect them to be more reluctant to use the courts to collect their accounts than their counterparts in cities where the business community frequently invoked government power to attain its objectives. Passive government and informal bargaining, typical of many public situations in Green Bay and Kenosha, also typified the debt collection process more frequently than in Madison and Racine. In Madison and Racine creditor-debtor conflicts, like public disputes, more frequently reached official government agencies (in this case, the courts) for formal adjudication.

The traditionalism we have spoken of spills over to the legal culture; the way in which attorneys handled garnishment cases in Green Bay indicated it. In Green Bay most attorneys sent letters to the debtors before initiating court action even though the cases referred to attorneys had already been extensively worked over by the creditor's collection department or a collection agency. Attorneys in no other city took this precaution, nor were they as concerned to avoid formal action. In the other cities most attorneys reported that when a file was given them, they immediately initiated court action unless they knew that no one else had tried to collect. The distaste of Green Bay attorneys for court action appears to reflect a more traditional, as well as conservative, attitude toward litigation. Lawyers in the other cities reflected the more modern view of litigation as a legitimate instrument to meet their objectives.

The differences in political culture among the four cities may also help explain the differences in bankruptcy usage. Most bankrupts were people who had learned about the procedure from friends and who found themselves in a supportive communication network. Fewer such supportive communications networks are likely to exist in traditional cities than in the more modern ones. Where public norms militate against taking private conflicts or problems to public arenas, this prohibition is likely to extend to bankruptcy proceedings as well as to other court actions. Furthermore, the very paucity of bankruptcy proceedings tends to reduce the number of communication linkages that might support the decision of newly insolvent debtors to resort to bankruptcy. The importance of the communication network in promoting bankruptcy lends significance to a public culture that might inhibit or promote such linkages. In Green Bay the traditional culture inhibited the growth of communication links that might have supported insolvent debtors' choice of bankruptcy as a remedy to their problems. Racine and Madison's more modern culture did not inhibit the growth of such networks.

conclusion

As with criminal proceedings, wide variations exist in the use of civil courts. Even when legislators make certain solutions equally available for all residents of their state, people choose to use them at varying rates. The variations appear to be linked to general characteristics of cities. If the experience of the four Wisconsin cities is a reliable guide, the same general process that delineates the style of politics in a city affects the way people use the courts. Where people are used to seeking public solutions to their common problems, they also appear more prone to use the courts for their private problems. In cities where they shun the public arena, people seek private settlement of their individual problems.

The link between city politics and civil court usage is more subtle than the links between city politics and criminal justice. The reason is that public officials play a prominent role in criminal justice; they play a much smaller role in the kind of civil cases we have examined in this chapter. It is significant, however, that even in such apparently private disputes as creditor-debtor conflicts, the political culture of a city substantially affects court use.

------------------------------ **notes** ------------------------------

1 Bankruptcy statistics are published annually by the Administrative Office of the United States Courts. In 1965, 180,000 bankruptcy petitions were filed. Garnishment statistics are published by some states. The present estimate is based on a count of garnishment actions in Wisconsin and is very conservative.

2 Estimates based on data in National Industrial Conference Board, *Economic Almanac, 1967–1968* (New York: The Macmillan Co., 1967), pp. 98, 457.

3 George Katona, *The Mass Consumption Society* (New York: McGraw-Hill Book Co., 1964).

4 "1967 Survey of Consumer Finances," mimeographed Statistical Report VIII (Ann Arbor: University of Michigan Survey Research Center), table VIII–1.

5 The following paragraphs draw heavily on George Katona, *The Mass Consumption Society*, especially pp. 1–8, 229–85; and on Robert Solomon, "The Changing Role of Consumption," in Board of Governors of the Federal Reserve System, *Installment Credit*, pt. I, vol. 1 (Washington, D.C.: Government Printing Office, 1957), pp. 7–21.

6 In 1967, 31 percent of all families had revolving accounts and 30 percent had gasoline credit cards; "1967 Survey of Consumer Finances," tables VIII–14 and VIII–15.

7 Hillel Black, *Buy Now, Pay Later* (New York: Pocket Books, Inc., 1962), pp. 84–96.

8 The cost of goods and credit is high in some low-income areas. See David Caplovitz, *The Poor Pay More* (New York: The Free Press, 1963), pp. 12–31.

9 National Industrial Conference Board, *Economic Alamanac*, pp. 98, 373.

10 "1967 Survey of Consumer Finances," table VIII–3.

11 For more details of this analysis, see Herbert Jacob, *Debtors in Court* (Chicago, Ill.: Rand McNally, 1969), p. 30.

12 The following is based in large part on Grant Gilmore, *Security Interests in Personal Property* (Boston, Mass.: Little, Brown & Company, 1965), vol. 1, pp. 62ff.

13 New federal regulations and statutes enacted in the 1970s have altered these proceedings to protect consumers more.

14 In legal parlance, garnishments are ancillary to the principal action, which is a suit to establish the legitimacy of the creditor's claims.

15 Among the court cases observed by the author, defendants appeared in less than 10 percent.

16 The procedure is detailed in chapter 267, Wisconsin Revised Statutes. See also Paul L. Moskowitz, *Wisconsin Garnishments and Exemptions* (Madison: University of Wisconsin Extension Law Department, 1962).

17 For a description of proceedings involved in Chapter 13 cases, see Miles C. Riley, "Chapter XIII's in Madison Bankruptcy Court," *Wisconsin Bar Bulletin*, 36 (February 1963), 10–13.

18 Both practices commonly occurred in Wisconsin in the mid-1960s.

19 Wis. Stat. Annotated, 272.18.

20 These exceptions are listed in ch. 3, sec. 17, of the Bankruptcy Act.

21 For details of the analysis leading to these measurements, see Jeffrey K. Hadden and Edgar D. Borgatta, *American Cities* (Chicago, Ill.: Rand McNally, 1965).

22 Robert R. Alford and Harry M. Scoble, "Urban Political Cultures," mimeographed (paper delivered at the meeting of the American Sociological Association, September 1964), pp. 1–5; quoted by permission of the authors. Elsewhere, the authors define *traditionalism* in terms of low professionalization with consequent informality in decision making and highly specialized leadership groups and also as a low degree of political participation (whether voluntary or involuntary). See Robert R. Alford with the collaboration of Harry M. Scoble, *Bureaucracy and Participation: Political Cultures in Four Wisconsin Cities* (Chicago, Ill.: Rand McNally, 1969). Some of the labels for the typology have been changed slightly.

crime, justice, and city politics: conclusions

*J*ustice has a unique position in city politics. It is indisputable that the quality of justice is important in determining the quality of life in the city. No one wants to live in imminent danger of suffering an injustice. It is equally clear that justice is a city-oriented value. It is not dispensed by some distant government in Washington or even from the state capital. It comes from officials working in local institutions responding in large part to local stimuli.

City governments appear to have little effective control over the delivery of justice, however. Even in the attempt to control crime, cities meet with little success. They have clear responsibility in this arena since most police forces are city agencies and ostensibly are controlled by city hall. But the disposition of criminal charges after arrest lies in the hands of court officials who respond to different guidelines than do the police. In addition, the police, like the courts, appear to concentrate on offenders whose criminal careers lie more in the past than in the future. Thus, they do not incarcerate the most productive criminals. Finally, the police learn about only a fraction of all crimes committed because most victims, for many reasons, do not call the police.

The activity of the police consequently has limited effect on the incidence of crime. Much of what the police do is symbolic activity to reassure the general public. For instance, in June 1978, several

Chicago Transit Authority (CTA) bus drivers were murdered. The incidents appeared to be random events; the drivers were killed by persons outside the buses rather than by passengers. The Chicago Transit Workers Union raised a great hue and cry over safety on public transportation, and the clamor was taken up by the media. Police officials explained that there was little they could do to prevent such incidents because it would require a police officer on each of the several thousand buses and trains run by the CTA as well as police officers at every bus stop and train station. Nevertheless, a token increase in the transit squad of the Chicago police was announced with considerable fanfare. No one who was knowledgeable about police patrols and crime incidence believed that the increase in patrols would "solve" the problem. If the public could be reassured that the transit system remained safe, however, the illusion of effective action would make the policy worthwhile and successful.

Symbolic successes are important because city officials often do not have more solid claims to success in fighting crime. Even when crime statistics drop, spectacular incidents rivet public attention on the potential danger of living in the city. Violent crimes are very personal. It is easy for people to empathize with the victims and their families. "There, but for the grace of God, go I" is what many people think when they read about a murder, rape, or kidnapping.

The personal nature of violent crime spreads its effect far beyond the actual victims. As we saw in the earlier chapters, most victims are poor, many are members of minority groups, most live in the city's ghettos and slums. For other problems—like welfare, education, housing, health, or transportation—the general result is benign neglect. Because these problems mostly affect the poor, the middle-class majority of a city tries to push the problems aside and use as little of the city's resources as possible to address them. Not so for crime. Crime, although in fact a problem of the poor, has been adopted by the rest of the city as its problem as well. Cities respond to the crime problem as if it were a problem for all citizens, not just principally one for the poor. Consequently, the police receive much more lavish attention than do teachers working in the ghettos. Cities pay police officers much more than social workers. They lay off street workers long before they reduce the size of their police departments. The illusion of public safety is more important to the quality of life than smooth streets or good English instruction in the schools.

Another point of confusion is that justice is not always served by an emphasis on public safety. There is wide agreement that persons guilty of offenses should be punished, but there is also a consensus that care must be taken to protect innocent persons from unjust accusations and convictions. One can never be certain that mistakes are not made. The likelihood of mistaken conviction may increase when most persons accused of crimes are induced to plead guilty rather than tried before judge or jury.

We do not, however, find much systematic discrimination against the poor or against minorities in the administration of criminal justice. Those accused of crimes receive the same treatment regardless of their race and wealth. Even those who have enough money to secure private attorneys do not receive substantially better treatment than those represented by public defenders or assigned counsel.[1] The principal qualification to these statements, however, is that most defendants are poor and a substantial minority (a plurality in some cities) are black. This results from the high incidence of crime among the poor and the concentration of law enforcement on crimes of violence and blue-collar property offenses instead of white-collar property crimes. Consequently, when we conclude that there is little discrimination against the poor or against minorities, we describe a situation in which there is little opportunity for discrimination since most defendants have the same socioeconomic characteristics. Nevertheless, this situation is far different from what prevails in the administration of civil justice.

Another problem in the administration of criminal justice is that punishments vary widely within and between cities. No particular group benefits or suffers from sentencing variations. Rather, variations occur within cities according to the predilections of judges and the bargaining situation in particular courtroom workgroups. Between cities, the variations appear to be related to regional value preferences. Sentencing variations exist amid a general lack of consensus about appropriate punishment for the guilty. The debate about punishment also takes place without the realization that those who are not convicted are also punished by their simple involvement as defendants in the criminal-prosecution process.

It is perhaps even more difficult to assess a city's performance in providing civil justice. As with criminal justice, there is no debate about the importance of civil justice to the quality of life in a city. No city is good to live in if one cannot get a fair deal in conflicts with landlords and merchants, if one cannot expect fair dealings after having been hit by a car, or if one cannot expect fair treatment in court in getting a divorce. But cities play a surprisingly modest role in assuring civil justice.

Civil justice has been largely privatized. Most remedies for private disputes are outside the governmental arena. Avoidance, negotiation, and mediation are generally the products of private decisions and private institutions. In addition, access to adjudication in public courts is controlled by the legal profession, whose actions are motivated by private incentives. City governments have traditionally been limited to providing support for courts that operate within a city's boundaries.

Civil justice discriminates against the poor more than against any other sector of society. Other people manage to take care of themselves or even to win outright gains. Segments of the business community, for example, capture the public courts and use them to their own advantage. Such discrimination does not alarm middle-class citizens in the same way that a crime wave does. Contrast the reaction to the crime wave against bus drivers in Chicago with the public's reaction to the exposé of Chicago's eviction court and its scandalous treatment of tenants. The eviction court report created little stir; it was greeted by a collective yawn from the media. After an initial denial of the problem, minor changes were promised but no visible public action was undertaken to assure the public that the court was being made as safe as the city's buses. Quite unlike criminal justice, civil justice has little general appeal to the public.

In addition, providing civil justice to the poor often means disadvantaging the powerful. Making eviction court fair means dealing more harshly with landlords. Making small-claims courts less biased means occasional rulings against merchants and collection agencies. Such actions mean that the city's commercial community will not be able to count on the courts as automatic extensions of their own interests. Because this is against their short-run goals, these commercial forces resist such changes. Their resistance usually succeeds since they have contacts with judges, influence with those who appoint or nominate court personnel, and resources to play the litigation game.

The neglect of justice by city governments is a political problem. It is a problem of mobilizing political resources and influence. The problem has been better solved at the national level than within individual urban areas.

At the national level much money has been poured into the criminal-justice process of cities, and some funds have also been allocated for the provision of civil justice. By far the largest amounts have gone to improve criminal justice. In 1960, the federal government spent 8 percent of all funds expended on criminal justice; in 1974, the federal share had risen to 13 percent, or almost $2 billion, with much of that money channeled to city governments.[2] A far smaller sum is now spent by the federal government to support legal-service clinics for the poor. Although those services remain inadequate in terms of both the number of people who remain unserved and the capability of the offices to render effective services, this federal initiative remains the most significant legal-service program for the poor in the United States. It operates almost entirely in urban areas, but with little local tax support.

Especially in the area of civil proceedings, cities have done little to alleviate the plight of the poor in obtaining justice. The reason is not that nothing can be done. Cities could help provide lawyers who would make it possible for poor people to defend themselves in court. Such legal services would also improve the ability of the poor to utilize other dispute-processing alternatives, particularly negotiation. When represented by an attorney and with adjudication as a credible threat, many poor persons with a just cause could win at the negotiating table. This is the experience of the legal-service clinics already in operation. They do not need to bring all of their cases to court; they can negotiate many of them to a reasonably successful conclusion.

In addition, cities could experiment much more fully with alternatives to adjudication. Establishing neighborhood justice centers that attempt to mediate disputes would provide another possibly effective alternative to adjudication for the poor. Almost without exception, these institutions, although located in cities, are supported by federal funds or by local philanthropies rather than by the city treasury. At best, cities tolerate such mediation centers; they have done little to encourage them.

With the fiscal crisis now facing most cities, it is perhaps understandable that they do not seek new programs that would claim scarce tax dollars. Yet there is no evidence that mediation institutions or legal-service clinics would prove especially costly. Nor is it established truth that such programs are less worthy of public support than many others that cities nourish. Many cities, for instance, are required by law to contribute to the salaries of judges and provide ancillary support to the courts that operate in their boundaries. Those, we have seen, largely provide for the welfare of the business community. An equal sum to make justice more available to disadvantaged members of the city could be equally well justified.

Such a program lacks the political support other policies have. The police usually assert themselves as a powerful lobby; they appeal to the general public. Education programs have a general appeal and are supported by teachers' and parents' organizations. Welfare programs are mandated by the federal government and have a considerable bureaucracy to mobilize support, although not from their clientele because welfare recipients are powerless and poor. Justice has no such lobby or organizational support. The only group to interest itself in justice continuously is the organized bar. In most cities the bar is dominated by the wealthiest lawyers, who have little interest in justice for the poor. Indeed, when lawyers perceive that a reform runs against their own self-interest—as many have with regard to no-fault automobile insurance—they oppose it even though the change might serve a broader dispensation of justice.

It is difficult to foresee the conditions under which this balance of interests and power would change enough to make civil justice a matter of higher priority for city governments. It is much more likely that civil justice will remain an area of neglect. The quality of justice in particular cities will remain more a function of their social structure and the accident of private initiatives than the product of their political processes.

notes

1 The evidence is summarized in Herbert Jacob, *Justice in America*, 3rd ed. (Boston, Mass.: Little, Brown & Company, 1978), pp. 185–86.

2 U.S. Department of Commerce, *Statistical Abstract of the United States, 1976* (Washington, D. C.: Government Printing Office, 1977), table 275.

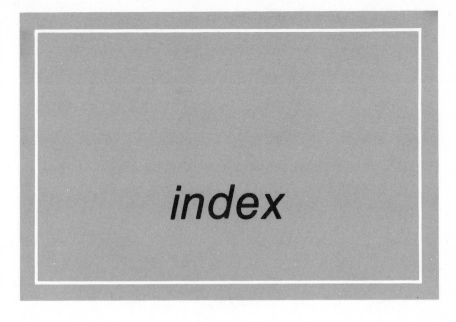

index